Written in a lively, accessible fashion and drawing extensively on interviews with people who were formerly incarcerated, *Cars and Jails* examines how the costs of car ownership and use are deeply enmeshed with the US prison system.

American consumer lore has long held the automobile to be a "freedom machine," consecrating the mobility of a free people. Yet, paradoxically, the car also functions at the crossroads of two great systems of entrapment and immobility—the American debt economy and the carceral state.

Cars and Jails investigates this paradox, showing how auto debt, traffic fines, over-policing, and automated surveillance systems work in tandem to entrap and criminalize poor people. The authors describe how racialization and poverty take their toll on populations with no alternative, in a country poorly served by public transport, to taking out loans for cars and exposing themselves to predatory and often racist policing.

Looking skeptically at the frothy promises of the "mobility revolution," Livingston and Ross close with provocative ideas for overhauling transportation justice, traffic policing, and auto-financing.

CARS AND JAILS

CARS AND JAILS

FREEDOM DREAMS, DEBT, AND CARCERALITY

JULIE LIVINGSTON AND ANDREW ROSS

with photographs
by Mychal Pagan

OR Books
New York · London

Published by OR Books, New York and London

Visit our website at www.orbooks.com

All rights information: rights@orbooks.com

First printing 2022

Cataloging-in-Publication data is available from the Library of Congress.
A catalog record for this book is available from the British Library.

Typeset by Lapiz Digital Services.

paperback ISBN 978-1-68219-349-5 • ebook ISBN 978-1-68219-350-1

Contents

Authors' Note

This book was researched and written under the auspices of the NYU Prison Education Program Research Lab, a subsidiary of the NYU Prison Education Program, which investigates the relationship between carcerality and debt. The Research Lab consists of a small group of faculty members, a postdoctoral fellow, and a rotating group of students who were formerly incarcerated, are trained in social science methods, and work as "peer researchers" within the project. Peer researchers pursue various modes of inquiry and expression including conducting oral interviews and producing video, photographic, and graphic materials, as well as social science scholarship.

The inspiration for *Cars and Jails*, and some of its content, is drawn from interviews conducted with formerly incarcerated men and women in the states of New York and Indiana by peer researchers and the authors. Due to the pandemic, the latter were conducted remotely. Quotations in the text are drawn from these interviews. We incurred our own debts while producing this book—first and foremost among them, to the past and present NYU Prison Education Program Research Lab members who contributed to this project from its inception: Tommaso Bardelli, José Diaz, Zach Gillespie, Derick McCarthy Jesus Meija, Mychal Pagan, Aiyuba Thomas, Vincent Thompson, and Thuy Linh Tu. We thank Michelle Daniel and Nick Greavan, who provided invaluable help in Indiana. Thanks are also due to Kaitlyn Noss, Marlene Brito, Raechel Bosch, and Nikhil Singh for support and assistance. Early results from this research were presented at the Seminar on Debt at the Committee on Globalization and Social Change at the CUNY Graduate Center, and we thank seminar members for their feedback and encouragement. We are grateful to Tanvi Kapoor and Tyler Bray who provided expert fact-checking. Thuy Linh Tu, Behrooz Ghamari-Tabrizi, and Tommaso Bardelli provided comments on the final draft. We thank the Center for Advanced Studies in the Behavioral Sciences at Stanford for providing support during the final phase of editing. Our gratitude goes to the OR Books team—Colin Robinson, Emma Ingrisani, and Acacia Handel—for making the production of this book a smooth, even enjoyable, experience. Finally and most importantly, we thank the interviewees who generously shared their time and expertise with us.

Police can choose from hundreds of traffic code violations to make a pretext stop and conduct a vehicle search.

Introduction

Every day more than fifty thousand Americans are pulled over by police officers while driving.[1] Most of them will come away from this encounter owing money to the municipality or county in which they were stopped. For some, the stop will culminate in their arrest—they will join the nearly nine million Americans who cycle through our country's jails each year.[2] At the other end of the system, more than six hundred thousand are released from prison annually. Typically, their first order of business is finding the means to get back behind the wheel of a car, which is an inescapable necessity in all but a few parts of the nation. Most will take on substantial financial liability to do so, joining their fellow motorists who owe more than $1.44 trillion in auto debt. American consumer lore has long held the automobile to be a "freedom machine," consecrating the mobility of a free people. Yet, paradoxically, the car also functions at the crossroads of two great systems of unfreedom and immobility—the credit economy and the American carceral system. This book investigates this paradox in detail, tracking how the long arms of debt and carcerality operate in tandem in the daily life of car use and ownership.

It is well known that people incarcerated in the US are disproportionately Black, brown, and poor, but there is much less recognition of the role played by automobiles in their incarceration. Here, then, is the cycle we take up in the following pages. Behind bars, incarcerated people mourn their lost mobility. They dream of cars they once owned and about cars in their future as a form of freedom. Upon release, they must drive as a basic necessity, but to do so have to take out auto loans on rapacious terms. Driving exposes them to costly traffic fines from police officers under orders to gin up revenue. A traffic stop, as a primary site of discretionary and racist policing, also opens them to potential arrest and reincarceration. If they are put back in the cage, they will lose their livelihood and all their assets in the process, including the equity in their car. Behind bars again, they start to dream once more about mobility and cars. This cycle does not always play itself out in its entirety or in such bald terms. Many people sidestep or break free from one or another of its traps. But tracking the steps in the cycle, as we do in this book, helps to illustrate *how* driving while Black or brown is both dangerous *and* expensive, as is driving while poor. It also helps expose how the financial system and American criminal justice collude with each other, whether inadvertently or through cold calculation.

We come to the car as part of a team that was formed to examine the impact of criminal justice debts on formerly incarcerated people.[3] As team members interviewed formerly incarcerated men and their family members in New York City about these debts, we noticed that the automobile appeared again and again.[4] Then one of our team was arrested while driving and reincarcerated for a minor parole violation. Soon that had happened to a second, and then also to a third formerly incarcerated person we had gotten to know in the course of our work. We began to see how the car was a key to the debt and carceral economies that interested us, and through it how poverty is wielded as a "secondary punishment" as well as a vehicle for profit-making. In subsequent interviews that we conducted ourselves, we decided to focus exclusively on car ownership and use, and this book draws heavily from them. We spoke to both men and women,[5] and while the majority of our interviewees were Black, we also spoke to a number of white and Latinx people. Most were located in either greater New York City (including New Jersey and Long Island) or in Indiana (mainly metro Indianapolis or the Gary/East Chicago area), though we did interview a few persons farther afield.

These people spoke fondly about their vehicles, and described the uphill battle of paying for them, while they also recalled fateful traffic stops or run-ins with police. The obvious pleasure they derived from their cars coexisted with an acute awareness of the perils of driving them. Over time, we uncovered more and more details about the connection between automobiles and incarceration: the loopholes used by police officers to circumvent bars on profiling and searches; the use of traffic citations to generate funding for local governments; the ability of debt collectors to manipulate the court system; the illegal deceptions employed by car dealers to ensnare consumers; and the requisitioning of prison labor to build roads and to make license plates. But we also concluded that car use and ownership are central to "carcerality at large." That is, the numerous ways in which discipline and control are exercised daily, far outside the prison or jailhouse walls, in ways that are redolent of the criminal justice system. These include the tyranny of the credit score, the expansion of data mining and scrutiny of individual conduct by government and corporations, the surveillance technologies built into cars, and the road warrior culture of a highly militarized society oriented to fossil fuel extraction and its procurement.

These constraints and other encounters with carcerality at large are not exceptional; they are routinely channeled through our purchase and operation of cars. Nor are they discretionary. For most of us, driving a car is non-optional. Despite mounting evidence that the auto-centric status quo poses serious threats to civil rights, financial sustainability, and planetary health, its maintenance is a central component of long-standing domestic and foreign policies. The right to freedom of movement is celebrated in countless ways in American culture, and most zealously in ad spots for cars whizzing along the open road. However, it is only referenced indirectly in the Constitution regarding the inviolable "privileges and immunities" of citizens, and it has had a spotty legal history of being honored.[6] Immigrant, homeless, Indigenous and other populations of color have never fully enjoyed the right to travel unchallenged, and the legions of future climate refugees are certain to face "roadblocks" and exclusionary zones. Most harshly, the free movement of African Americans, from 1619 onward, has been cruelly denied, rolled back, or relentlessly monitored. Even the general public saw travel between states curtailed during the pandemic lockdown, while the explosive growth of state and commercial surveillance has meant that more and more of our movements are tracked, dissected, and channeled on a daily basis.

The disparity between the heady rhetoric of the open road and its compromised reality is most visible in the regulation and profiling of private motorists by police officers. In the early twentieth century, automobile boosters fought a bitter war with pedestrians to win the "right of way." During that fight, they fervently invoked the rallying cry of unrestricted freedom of passage. Yet their success was offset by calls for traffic enforcement in the name of public safety. The outcome was the invention of modern policing—a mobile street apparatus embroiled from the outset in legal conflict over the constitutionality of warrantless searches of vehicles. The right of police officers to interrupt traffic and infringe on free movement was quickly conceded by the courts (*Carroll vs. United States*, 267 U.S. 132 [1925]) on the basis that private cars operating on public roads did not merit the privacy protections accorded to pedestrians or to residents in their homes. Over time, the pretextual traffic stop—in which an officer pulls over a vehicle to conduct a speculative criminal investigation unrelated to the traffic code—became an increasingly common feature of motorized travel. The volume of stops swelled from the 1970s, as a result of the War on Drugs, and later in response to top-down pressure from local governments seeking to extract revenue from traffic fines and associated court fees. This invasive policing practice cast a long shadow over the civil rights landscape, consigning millions to jails and prisons, and resulting in the deaths of numerous Black drivers at the hands of trigger-happy officers.

By mid-century, African American car owners had more reason than anyone to see their vehicles as "freedom machines." They savored the newfound means to escape, however temporarily, from redlined urban ghettos in the North or segregated towns in the South. But they quickly found their progress on roads outside of the metro core regularly obstructed by police, threatened by vigilante assaults, and stymied by owners of whites-only restaurants, lodgings, and gas stations. By the turn of the twenty-first century, "driving while Black" had become a well-traveled route to incarceration, or the raison d'être for gratuitous police violence. These hazards had also been supplemented by the menace of debt servitude as the costs of financing and maintaining a car ballooned. As with other debt classes, the economic burden, not to mention the potential legal jeopardy, of high-interest auto loan payments falls disproportionately on low-income and BIPOC owners. Anyone can end up in jail if they are too poor to pay.

But to fully understand how the hazards and thrills of the open road evolved in tandem with one another, we need to understand how the roads came to be where they are. If we want to reimagine a system of transportation that is just, we must first see the current one as the product of a set of deliberate decisions rather than the outcome of natural technological development.

The Finality of the Federal Road Map

Funding a massive program to repair and modernize the national infrastructure was the one big idea to break free from the gridlock of the federal government during the Trump and Biden administrations. Trump's contribution amounted to little more than lip service, but Biden's $2.5 trillion proposal, unveiled as the American Jobs Plan in March 2021, was sweeping in scope and purpose. It was billed as a one-time, public "investment in America" that promised to upgrade not only the transportation network, but almost every sector of the *real* economy—commerce, education, health care, housing, water, energy, communications, R&D, logistics, labor, and the environment.

There was something in it for everyone, including some red meat for foreign policy hawks—the plan, according to the White House, would "position the United States to out-compete China." Apparently, summoning the public spirit of "great projects of the past" like the space program and the interstate highway required a modern adversary with global heft comparable to the Soviet threat. The American Jobs Plan named two "great challenges of our time"—"the climate crisis and the ambitions of an autocratic China," a country which had embarked on its own, much more extensive, infrastructure program, Belt and Road.[7] Ever since World War II thrust the US into a permanent war economy, the prospects for large-scale federal spending programs have been boosted if they were couched in the form of declarations of war like the War on Poverty, War on Drugs, War on Crime, or War on Terror.

Biden's team issued an ersatz version of this belligerent rhetoric, falling far short, for example, of designating global climate change as an emergency that requires all hands on deck. But that was not the only problem with their policy pitch. Compared to the heyday of federal power in the 1950s and 1960s, when states eagerly aligned with Washington to approve the first forty-one thousand miles of the interstate highway network, the business of federal politics has become a hot mess, more prone to giving up regulatory power than to exercising it for some large progressive goal.

Despite its 2,700-page length, the $1.2 trillion bill (Infrastructure Investment and Jobs Act) that emerged six months later from the Congressional sausage machine was lean and mean.[8] The rewriting of appropriations for transportation needs was all too revealing. The sums initially proposed for rail and public transit had been sliced by nearly half, while funding for new roads and bridges designed for private vehicle use survived almost intact. Shredding the hopes of those who were counting on a more even-handed distribution between drivers and transit agencies, the final split (82/18) was even worse than the 80/20 ratio observed by congressional custom since the years of the first Nixon administration.[9] Even though the auto industry has begun to see that its future lies in electric power, the fossil fuel lobby succeeded in downsizing or stripping out many of the provisions for electric vehicles (EV)—including consumer incentives and charging stations. Transportation is the largest contributor to greenhouse gas emissions in the US, exceeding industry, buildings, and agriculture, and so the decision to lock in personal car use as the bill's central component may prove to be just as ruinous as the Cold War programs that gave birth to the national auto-centric landscape.

The bipartisan group that hashed out the infrastructure bill also gutted a $20 billion program for reconnecting predominantly Black and brown neighborhoods that had been broken apart by urban freeways. The final version allocated a paltry $1 billion to the task of highway removal (more likely to be used to build pedestrian bridges), snubbing community advocates who have documented the ongoing harms generated by these roads in the form of pollution, social isolation, and economic deprivation. It was also a slap in the face for Pete Buttigieg, the secretary of transportation, who caused a stir by suggesting that "there is racism physically built into some of our highways," adding that their impact "wasn't just an act of neglect," but also a "conscious choice."[10]

How conscious was that choice? Timing was a key component. Legal scholar Deborah Archer has pointed out that these urban highways were built at a time when "courts around the country were striking down traditional tools of racial segregation." Just as the "possibility of integration in housing was on the horizon," the federal bulldozer not only ruthlessly rammed through neighborhoods, it also followed boundary lines that had been used previously for racial zoning, and sometimes directly at the behest of white community members concerned about encroachment by Black households into their all-white residential neighborhoods.[11] The highways that connected Cold War suburban commuters to center-city workplaces served as new segregationist barriers and, in many cities, they carry on that fateful concrete legacy to this day.[12]

If it had lived up to the name of its authorizing legislation, the National System of Interstate and Defense Highways Act (1956), the interstate highway system would have given cities a wide berth, since they were prime targets of nuclear warfare. But the bill's military rationale of building a road network in the service of rapidly transporting troops and ordnance around the country was only a piece of salesmanship. The highways were destined to serve commerce and land development on the urban fringe, and so they ended up connecting cities, just as arterial roads and railways had done. Even if they were aligned with the permanent war economy in name only, the interstates were planned and standardized with military precision, and they primed the pump of consumption as efficiently as Cold War expenditure did for the defense industries.

The origins of an intercontinental, all-weather road system can be traced to the grand project of the 620-mile National Road, or Cumberland Road (which forms part of U.S. Route 40 today). It was built with great fanfare by the federal government between 1811 and 1837 to connect the Potomac and Ohio Rivers, and to serve as a thoroughfare for waves of western-bound settlers who had been pouring through the Cumberland Gap for several decades. Indeed, the road, which followed an Indigenous trail, was first proposed by Thomas Jefferson, after his purchase of the Louisiana Territory opened new lands west of the Mississippi for settlement.[13] By the time President Eisenhower brokered the Federal Highway Act, a vast highway lobby had sprung into existence to push for a national network. Almost as powerful as the "military-industrial complex" which he warned about, this coalition consisted of the industrial interests of oil, cement, steel, rubber, real estate, automobiles, asphalt, agriculture, construction, tourism, and, last but not least, trucking. Also known as the "road gang," their combined influence on lawmakers has historically resulted in the measly allocations of federal dollars for public transit.[14]

The new limited-access highways transformed patterns of settlement much more radically than the canals and railroads before them. Though the forces that steered mass suburbanization were already in the driver's seat, the interstates accelerated the population shift outward from rail-served urban centers, spawning low-density subdivisions, with single-use zoning, all along their asphalt connector routes. Ironically, it was George F. Kennan, the key diplomatic architect of Cold War containment, who issued one of the most stinging early critiques:

> The automobile ... has turned out to be, by virtue of its innate and inalter-able qualities, the enemy of community generally. Wherever it advances, neighborliness and the sense of community are impaired ... One might have thought that this alone, much of which was surely becoming evident in the 1920s and 1930s, would have sufficed to cause Americans of that day to pause and to ask themselves whether they really wished to junk 99 percent of the great railway system that then existed and to confer upon the automobile and the truck the sort of near monopoly on transportation which ... they have now achieved.[15]

The junking of Kennan's beloved railroads, whose stations and terminals anchored the cities and dictated their compact settlement patterns, along with the trolley car systems that connected many prewar suburbs, was by no means inevitable. After all, high-volume passenger and freight rail survived and thrived in many other countries through programs of nationalization or strong government subsidies. But in the US, rail travel was almost wholly in private hands (until Amtrak was launched in 1971) and owners had seen falling profits for some time. Its advocates were comprehensively outgunned by the Road Gang.

The new freeways enthroned cars and trucks as the sovereign transportation mode. Private vehicles were now unrestricted in their movement from coast to coast, and to all points in between (interstates were also built in noncontiguous territories like Hawaii and Puerto Rico). This all-access domain brought the settler colonial dream of complete geographic mobility within reach. Inevitably, eulogies for this feat of independence from natural topography gave way to bluster about the superiority of the American Way, symbolized by the freedom machines churned out by the auto industry. Streamlined and loaded with gadgetry and baroque styling—including elaborate tailfins, deep-pile upholstery, power steering, padded interiors, wraparound windshields, fanged grills, fake gun ports, pastel paint jobs, and oodles of surplus chrome—Detroit's mass-produced showpiece was the poster child for the Free World during the early decades of the Cold War.[16]

The flipside of this much-vaunted autonomy over movement was a widespread *dependence* on the automobile itself. The deconcentration of population and industry meant that car ownership was increasingly a necessity for many. The optional or voluntary element of automotive liberty segued into compulsory use. In the new auto-centric landscape, access to employment, retail, hospitals, schools, and recreational amenities would become impossible for those without costly personal vehicles. Over time, the need to perform these daily tasks gave rise to the multiple-car household. Almost 60 percent of US households now have at least two cars, while less than 9 percent have no access to a car. The average American motorist spends close to eighteen days per year driving a car, most of that time alone, and increasingly performing their jobs remotely while in their vehicles, through advanced communications. Even in the few cities with robust transit systems, like New York, a large percentage of jobs are not easily accessible by trains or buses.

This dependence takes a heavy economic toll. Transportation accounts for one-fifth of household budgets, with low-income car owners the hardest hit. Some of our interviewees paid much more for transportation than housing. One man with whom we spoke put it simply—"a car is a bill." Financialization of the auto sector has added to the burden. After household incomes stagnated in the 1970s and '80s, financing a car purchase was the only option available. Today, of the 85 percent of buyers who have to borrow to secure a new vehicle, more than one in six takes out a subprime loan at high interest rates, and many end up owing more than their car is worth.[17] A chronic lack of regulation has allowed fraud and deception to permeate the business of auto financing. By the estimate of one former car dealer, 65 percent of auto loans involved deceptive and predatory practices.[18] So, too, the repossession and collection industries rely on courts to threaten arrest and detention for those who cannot pay. Though debtors' prisons were abolished in 1833, borrowers who can't keep up with their payments can still end up behind bars, effectively criminalized for their poverty.

This state of auto-dependence and debt servitude is a direct consequence of public policy that sidelined public transit, deregulated finance, and green-lighted development beyond the urban fringe. In crafting legislation and allocating budgets, policymakers were heavily swayed by the highway lobby, Wall Street's campaign contributions, and the land development industry, with its own powerful lobby. Little was left to chance, or to the free choice of consumers.

Detroit, Wall Street, and Silicon Valley

The auto industry no longer lies at the dynamic heart of the US economy. Finance and high tech can now claim to be more important drivers. Forty-five percent of cars sold in the American market are made by a foreign brand (with majority percentages in many coastal states). But the legacy of Detroit's heyday—when one in six American jobs depended on cars (today it is less than one in twenty), and when "what's good for GM" was "good for America"—is still far-reaching and unavoidable. Unlike the telecommunications infrastructure, which has been transformed by digital technologies, the road system created to host the country's number one commodity has not been easy to modify, let alone repurpose.

Despite the changing demography of the suburban social order to which it gave birth, the apartheid character of the auto-centric Cold War landscape laid out by the GI Bill, the interstate highways, racist housing policies, and the long arm of Jim Crow has left its mark in ways that are recognizable today. The appreciation of housing equity earned by white suburban households over the last sixty years is one of the largest contributors to the racial wealth gap—the net worth of the median white household is almost ten times greater than its Black counterpart.[19] Persistent segregation across the residential landscape means that Black Americans must drive longer distances to access workplaces. Due to blatant discrimination, they also pay more for auto loans and insurance, and they incur traffic fines, license suspensions, and court fees much more often than their white counterparts.[20]

We continue to live in a polity where social status is advertised by the make and model of the cars we drive. When consumer capitalism rebounded and mushroomed after the war, its boosters preached the doctrine that status, expressed through incremental material improvements, had replaced class consciousness and conflict. Moving up the ladder of social standing was most visibly demonstrated by the smooth progression of ownership from a Chevrolet to a Buick, and then a Cadillac, while the spectrum of available models distinguished the American Way from the standardized vehicles of the socialist bloc. (East Germany's Trabant was unchanged for thirty years.) Today's highly customized marketplace has much more variety, and while cars are sold as much on the premise that they reflect our "personality," vehicle choice remains an all-important marker of individual worth.

So, too, civic identity in the US is most often validated by proof of a state-issued license to drive. This is only feasible because car ownership was promoted as a universal goal, if not a birthright, of American citizenship. In 1906, when cars were still widely resented as elite objects of conspicuous consumption, Woodrow Wilson darkly proclaimed that "nothing has spread socialistic feeling more than the use of the automobile." But by 1929, the aspiration for mass democratic ownership was being evoked in Herbert Hoover's presidential campaign promise of "a chicken in every pot . . . and a car in every backyard."[21] Although half of American households possessed a car by the mid-1930s, fuller delivery on that promise was delayed by the Great Depression. But in the decade after the auto factories finally converted from wartime production, sales quadrupled, and the automobile market was within sight of its saturation point. Acquisition of a driver's license became a rite of passage for youth, and a mark of adult citizen-belonging. As the most widely recognized personal credential, it was preferred over a national identity card, associated in libertarian minds with totalitarian countries. By that same token, lack of a license carries significant social disadvantages. Most recently these include being disenfranchised in many states that have passed voter ID laws to challenge the eligibility of Black and Latinx people, who are less likely to possess licenses.

The high-velocity world bequeathed by the interstates bypassed much of rural America. Indeed, traveling on some rural roads can make us imagine that the hinterlands of furrowed fields, silos, red barns, and well-weathered farmhouses are largely untouched by modernity. However, chances are that the bucolic scenery will soon yield to the view of an unsightly penitentiary building ringed by razor wire and guard towers; fellow travelers on that road are likely to include van drivers transporting incarcerated people from urban jails. For the last forty years, prisons have been a primary growth industry for rural areas hit by farm foreclosures and population loss. As rates of incarceration rose by 500 percent over that period, rural communities actively and desperately sought out government investment in penitentiaries as a development strategy, though the results do not show sustained beneficial impacts.[22] Employment in these areas came to depend on criminal courts maintaining a steady supply of convicted offenders. But a primary point of capture for incarcerated people is through the traffic stop, an interaction between police and drivers that evolved, along with the road network, into a menacing ritual. As noted earlier, and according to the Stanford Open Policing Project, police pull over more than twenty million motorists annually, with significantly skewed patterns of racial bias.[23] The fact is that policymakers who approved the basic funds and subsidies for the auto-centric infrastructure also passed laws for policing it that have imprisoned millions.

The roads and highways built during the postwar development boom remain mostly unchanged, but the automotive world of the twenty-first century has been transformed in other ways. According to Kelley Blue Book, in September 2021, the average transaction price for a light vehicle in the United States broke the $45,000 mark, far beyond the direct consuming range of most households.[24] Financing that kind of purchase has moved into the forefront of the auto marketplace, with the advent of exploitative instruments like seven-year loans, deep subprime borrowing, and the practice of leasing cars to customers who will never own them. As early as the 1930s, General Motors discovered that GMAC, its financing arm, was more profitable than its retail business, but over the last decade the tail has begun to wag the dog. The advent of an auto-loan-backed securities market is now helping to drive sales, especially in the high-risk subprime category. By the second quarter of 2022, the average amount financed for new vehicles surpassed $40,000, while the equivalent figures for used cars surpassed $30,000 earlier in the year.[25] In May 2022, the average monthly car payment climbed above $700 for the first time, and total auto debt ballooned to $1.47 trillion.[26] The car that almost everyone needs has become one of the most tightly sprung debt traps, contributing in no small measure to the criminalization of poverty for those unable to keep up with their monthly payments.

The auto industry's bet on the future of greener production models is its latest opportunity for profitable reinvention. Electric and hybrid vehicles, currently 7 percent of the cars owned in the US, may well wean drivers off a high-carbon lifestyle tied to the nineteenth-century technology of the internal combustion engine.[27] EV maintenance costs are lower, but if the long-standing habit of personal ownership retains its edge over car sharing, it is unlikely that new generations of vehicles will lighten the rampant auto debt load. The rise of EVs, and the holy grail of driverless cars, are not the only radical shifts in automotive engineering; automobiles are increasingly equipped with built-in sensors and computers generating a host of data. But this "connected car" is already triggering alarms about privacy violations. In many new car models with advanced technology, data is collected by the onboard computers and transmitted back to carmakers in volumes of up to twenty-five gigabytes per hour. Information about vehicle location, vehicle performance, and driver behavior is gathered through the telematics system, while plugging a smartphone into a car's infotainment system will result in the transmission of personal data. What carmakers do with all the data is entirely their business and currently not subject to regulation.[28]

Civil liberties groups are concerned about the sale of data to corporations and government agencies, including law enforcement.[29] Police officers in fully connected cruisers now have the potential to access all kinds of personal information forensically extracted from our smart car systems and entered into government databases. The ability to rapidly process this information presents an opportunity to circumvent constitutional prohibitions against unreasonable searches. Even before we are pulled over, officers already know a lot about us from our license plate numbers, which are portals to these data troves.

To put it bluntly, our next-generation cars are watching us. They are still sold to us as freedom machines, offering a high-velocity respite from the constraints and pressures of our overcommitted lives. But they are also functioning as key branches of networked surveillance, with data supplied from the stealth systems hidden beneath their consoles or accessed by commercial license plate readers that are now being marketed to homeowner associations and private individuals. The breadth and scale of this surveillance demonstrates the advance of the carceral state far beyond the precincts of prisons, jails, and courts.

A Holistic Approach

Readers of this book may be familiar with some topics we cover, whether they concern traffic stops, revenue policing from fines and fees, the overreach of surveillance, the auto loan business, criminal justice debt, or the profound racial bias running through any of these. We have decided to take a holistic approach that incorporates almost all of them. Our reason for that choice is because these issues run together in the lives of the people we interviewed, so it made little sense to separate their impacts. Car trouble and car pleasure were woven into each of their stories, loosely anchored by their daily struggle to balance needs and resources while rebuilding a post-carceral life.

Reform advocates tend to focus on single issues, and operate within different domains of the law. For example, those concerned about the injustices of auto loan debt, which is adjudicated in small claims or civil courts, appeal to consumer law. Others focus on debt generated by traffic violations. This is dealt with in traffic or even criminal courts, and they have to grapple with state law. But from the perspective of households juggling multiple debt service obligations, the distinction between traffic and auto loan debt doesn't matter much, especially when either can result in jail time. So, while we devote chapters to each of these topics, in addition to the spread of surveillance and the checkered history of traffic policing, the goal of *Cars and Jails* is to capture how they all overlap in the lives of drivers vulnerable to predatory targeting. In other words, our holistic approach illustrates how carcerality and creditocracy work in concert.

The state is a creditor in the case of traffic debt, for which it is also an enforcer and adjudicator. Yet governments, which regulate and extract revenue from many other aspects of the operation of vehicles (licenses, registrations, plates, and titles) minimize their oversight responsibilities when it comes to consumer debt racked up by automobile use and purchase. We take issue with this lopsided division of duties, and with the corresponding abdication of the state's obligation to adequately regulate. Cars are not like other market commodities; in the US they are a basic need, required for everyday life. Decades of preferential government policy are largely responsible for the financial and legal liabilities faced by drivers daily. A fuller acknowledgement of the state's role should lead to much stronger protection and innovative transportation alternatives, through tougher commercial regulation, decriminalization, and the provision of attractive public transit options.

In addition to our interviews with, and guidance from, formerly incarcerated persons, this book draws from investigative journalism, NGO studies and reports, peer scholarship, and state data archives. Our findings are relevant to many areas of policy—transportation, commerce, environment, defense, and criminal justice—because the purchase, use, and policing of cars is so central to what people mean by the American way of life. They also show how deeply ingrained the pattern of racial bias is.

One of the most iconic commentaries on the uneven, racialized delivery of American auto-consumerism is Margaret Bourke-White's famous 1937 photo of African American men, women, and children lined up outside a relief agency in the wake of a disastrous Kentucky flood. Above them looms a billboard for the National Association of Manufacturers depicting a smiling white family of four (and their dog) riding in a car under a banner bearing the slogan "World's Highest Standard of Living. There's no way like the American Way." It may seem glib, but it is also irresistible, to imagine a dystopian twenty-first-century version of the image in which the people in the car are African American, and they are paying 25 percent APR compounded monthly on an overpriced car in order to drive on an open, rural road to visit a relative in prison.

Car decal referencing the film *Transformers*—a twist on the original LAPD motto, "to protect and serve."

Chapter One

The Right to Mobility?

Every so often, media headlines invite readers to consider whether Americans' *love affair with cars* is over. Typically, the occasion for such stories is a significant decline in auto sales, the kind of drop logged most recently during the Great Recession, and then again during the pandemic lockdown. But sometimes the context is more disruptive and system-wide, as in the imminent "mobility revolution" of car- and ridesharing, which heralds a future beyond private ownership. Or in the prospect of the driverless vehicle, which may finally extinguish the romance of being behind a wheel.

In truth, the death of automobility as we know it has been proclaimed many times before; most notably after the Golden Age of Detroit streamline styling ended, and then again after environmentalists sounded the alarm about carbon emissions and began to promote smarter transit.[1] Each time, the auto industry has surged back. After the mass rollout of SUVs and pickups in the 1990s, these gas-guzzlers made inroads on the market, outdoing sedan sales by 2015, and outselling them by two to one only four years later.[2] At the time of writing, the widespread decision of carmakers to back electric vehicles—the preferred method for automobile propulsion in the late nineteenth and early twentieth centuries, before the oil industry drove the dominance of internal combustion—looks like a winning strategy to accelerate the industry back out of the pandemic slump.[3]

America's most important industrial commodity no longer commands a dominant position within the economy as a provider of jobs. Nor are cars so extensively used—the number of miles traveled per person and household peaked in 2004,[4] and the rise of online shopping and remote work will no doubt result in a further decline. But the car's status as an *inescapable* asset for the majority of American households has barely diminished. Almost 90 percent of these households simply could not function without one, and many require two cars (1.88 cars per household on average) to meet their everyday needs and obligations.[5]

The reasons for this dependence are circular in nature. The infrastructure of twentieth-century urban growth was laid down to facilitate automobile travel, and the result was hardwired—few households can now navigate this asphalt landscape without a car. For most Americans, commutes to employment, retail, and recreation are otherwise inaccessible. None of this was inevitable—a formidable coalition of carmakers, oil companies, land developers, highway and housing builders, tire and steel manufacturers, and others lobbied hard for massive federal subsidies to terraform the metro hinterland into an automotive environment. Despite all the evidence that this coalition's preferred path of profitable growth is ecologically destructive, it has not been easy to deflect, let alone retrofit. Indeed, the recent surge of investment in electric cars, dependent on a widespread highway network of charging stations, seems guaranteed to extend the life of this infrastructure.

So, if auto ownership is all but mandatory, where does the American "love affair" with the car fit in? How is it possible that so many of our interviewees described cars as a "necessity" and a "luxury" in the same breath? And what does this tell us about how financialization has come to propel carcerality and vice versa? These questions cannot be fully answered unless we understand how automobility has been so central to the history of racial capitalism.

Groucho Marx may have been first to use the phrase "love affair" while shilling for DuPont and General Motors in the 1961 TV documentary *Merrily We Roll Along* about the early decades of American motoring, and it has been a commonplace ever since. Yet Peter Norton, Clay McShane, and other historians of those fledgling years have established that love had little to do with it. In their accounts, the conquest of urban and rural space was a bitter, and sometimes violent, class war of stone-throwing and gun-toting pedestrians against well-heeled motorists for whom driving was a prestige pursuit. As part of the campaign to win the "right of way" for cars, dissident pedestrians were demonized by industry pressure groups, and eventually criminalized as "jaywalkers."[6]

By the mid-1920s, the market had grown far beyond the orbit of hoity-toity metropolitan elites. Car possession was firmly established as a basic necessity for the masses, even in small towns like Muncie, Indiana, immortalized by Robert and Helen Lynd in their classic 1929 study *Middletown*:

> "We'd rather do without clothes than give up the car," said one mother of nine children. "We used to go to his sister's to visit, but by the time we'd get the children shoed and dressed there wasn't any money left for [street] carfare. Now no matter how they look, we just poke 'em in the car and take 'em along."[7]

According to another Middletown resident, "We don't have no fancy clothes when we have the car to pay for ... the car is the only pleasure we have." Yet another declared: "I'll go without food before I'll see us give up the car."[8]

Madison Avenue had something to do with the rapid nationwide distribution of the more popular models from Studebaker, Nash, Hudson, and Packard, in addition to Ford, General Motors, and Chrysler. But the existential priority that Middletowners placed on their automobiles was no false need fabricated by the admen.[9] And the pleasure that car possession afforded to those living in humble circumstances was quite unlike the novelty thrill generated by a consumer bauble. Utilitarian reliance on their vehicles was a given, and the cars were coveted. If there was a romance involved, the kernel of a love affair, then it fed off the fever of modernity, maybe even the fast promise of status, but more likely because the car offered a ready escape from their immediate, often humdrum, surroundings.

The Madison Avenue persuaders were able to run with that felt freedom and fashioned it into a compelling doctrine of consumption.[10] The privacy afforded by the automobile was easily played off against the inconveniences of mass transit, with undertones of anti-socialist messaging. Less subtle than the admen, industry trade groups converted this benefit into a full-blown ideology of national belonging. "Americans are a race of independent people," pronounced the vice president of the National Chamber of Commerce, "their ancestors came to this country for the sake of freedom and adventure. The automobile satisfies these instincts."[11] Rhetoric like this provided cover for the campaign on the part of the auto-oil-rubber coalition to take over the sprawling public streetcar systems of Los Angeles and other US cities and replace their tracks with bus and auto routes.[12] As the Cold War progressed, these paeans to the libertarian birthright of capitalist democracy got louder and more elaborate. In the early years of the twentieth century, regulations, such as speed limits, introduced for public safety were derided as socialist plots. When seat belts and emission control devices were introduced by federal mandate in 1967 and 1970 respectively, they were assailed as the coercive moves of an authoritarian state trampling on open-throttle liberties. Inevitably, during the Trump administration, a Department of Transportation and the Environmental Protection Agency joint initiative to roll back Obama-era car fuel economy standards was ballyhooed as "Make Cars Great Again."

Ideology aside, the freedoms associated with cars were welcomed for many reasons, and not just because automobility allowed access to a world beyond the suburban settlement patterns that mandated a need to drive everywhere. Cars were prized for ease of navigation across and through the built-up environment but also for the heady rush of release onto the open road. Cruising, joyriding, and backseat sexual initiation became rites of passage for postwar youth, and, for the elderly, the ability to get out and about was a deliverance from loneliness and isolation. Access to the car, for restless flappers, or postwar suburban wives trapped in their dream homes, was also a reprieve, if not exactly an instrument for women's liberation.[13] After all, suburban infrastructure was designed to serve highly gendered needs, where female access to a car was central to the everyday tasks of social reproduction, most evident in daily trip-chaining.[14] As for men, the primary target of the auto sales industry, they acquired personal control over a powerful machine, whereas their daily jobs had made them the subjects of mechanical domination. And for those who learned how to customize their vehicles—including several generations of hotrodders, dragsters, and lowriders—there was the sovereignty of expression through craft styling or reengineering. Wherever conformity, confinement, and anomie reigned, cars were the getaway vehicle.

The road movie at its best—*It Happened One Night* (1934), *Sullivan's Travels* (1941), *Detour* (1945), *Voyage in Italy* (1953), *Pierrot le Fou* (1965), *Bonnie and Clyde* (1967), *Easy Rider* (1969), *Five Easy Pieces* (1970), *Two-Lane Blacktop* (1971), *Badlands* (1973), *Alice in the Cities* (1974), *Thieves Like Us* (1974), *Paris, Texas* (1984), *Stranger Than Paradise* (1984), *Thelma and Louise* (1991), *My Own Private Idaho* (1991), *Natural Born Killers* (1994), *The Adventures of Priscilla, Queen of the Desert* (1994), *Y tu mamá también* (2001), *Queen & Slim* (2019), and *Nomadland* (2020)—captures the redemptive spirit of taking off for parts unknown, even when the trip ends, as it often does, in oblivion.

Queen & Slim features a young Black couple on the run after accidentally killing a racist cop who pulls them over for a minor traffic violation. They are on their way home after their first, and what looks like their last, date. The romance between them takes root on the road as they survive a series of close brushes with the law, until their luck runs out. In this genre, any kind of transgression can set a fugitive road trip in motion, but it is almost foreordained that a prejudicial traffic stop would trigger a tragic love narrative about African Americans in vehicular motion. While the film spins a poignant tale about folk heroism from these circumstances, the fateful encounter with the cop resonates with the long and perilous history of driving while Black.

Filmmakers are fond of featuring traffic stops by police—they are a ready source of drama, with the potential for conflict and mayhem. Still, it is rare to see these setups, however routine, portrayed as racialized interactions with fatal consequences. Ironically, this visual standpoint has become more familiar to us through raw video footage of such encounters from police car dashboards, officer body cameras, or bystanders' cell phones. The ominous approach of the armed deputy is inexorably followed by some indeterminate response on the driver's part, and the woeful sound of shots being fired. When it comes to the business of speaking candidly about the fraught experience of African American motorists, Hollywood is a nonstarter compared to the cinema verité provided by these nonprofessional sources.

The jury is (literally) still out on how effective this relatively new supply of evidence will be in combating the abuse of police powers. But there is no doubt that it has boosted public awareness about the routine limitations placed on Black and brown drivers when it comes to enjoying the freedoms of auto-citizenship. The virtues of the open road long touted by auto industry boosters were imagined primarily on behalf of white consumers, relatively unrestricted and unsurveilled in their range of movement. No such privilege was guaranteed to minority customers, even though the cars were promoted to them based on the same allure. Nor was there any innocence in that freedom of movement, once attained. For when they joined the ranks of drivers speeding blithely across unceded land, the brands they drove bearing American Indian names—Pontiacs, Chevrolet Apaches, Dodge Dakotas, Jeep Cherokees, Ford Thunderbirds, and Winnebagos— could rightfully be seen through Indigenous eyes as symbols of conquest.[15]

Black Mobility

The story of restricted freedom of movement for African Americans originates in the shackles of the slave trade and continues through the many afterlives of slavery. By corollary, the genesis of American policing lies in the "slave patrol," first organized in the Carolina (1704) and Virginia (1727) colonies in the early eighteenth century. The aim of the patrol was to chase down runaways, monitor the system of passes allowing slave-workers to move between plantations, and crack down on slave gatherings, educational materials, and any signs of resistance.[16] These functions were reinforced, and formalized, under the Fugitive Slave Acts of 1793 and 1850, and in the vagrancy laws of the South's Black Codes. The patrolling practices were kept alive and elaborated in postbellum police departments and through the rank and file of the Ku Klux Klan. While convict leasing and chain gangs built the road networks of the South, its violent Jim Crow order was carefully organized around rules and laws inhibiting the movement of African Americans and their occupation of space.

White anxiety about Black mobility was especially heightened around shared access to public transportation, and so it was no coincidence that *Plessy v. Ferguson*, the seminal 1896 Supreme Court ruling that established the "separate but equal" doctrine of segregation, stemmed from the refusal of Homer Plessy, an African American train passenger, to sit in the separate Black car. The advent of Black automobile ownership was a genuine release from the indignity and injustice of segregated travel, and so the freedoms offered to African Americans by private motoring were qualitatively different from those experienced by white drivers. And for Black women in particular, car ownership offered potential protection from the catcalls and threat of sexual violence they experienced on foot from white men trolling Southern streets in their Chevys.[17] The newfound ability to venture far beyond the badly paved streets of Jim Crow communities had its correlate in the North, where redlining had consolidated the spatial constraints of the urban ghetto and where highways that serviced white flight commuters were rammed through inner-city neighborhoods. For Black Americans with access to private cars, the journey out of town was like a jailbreak from the social confines of urban apartheid and led to places that were inaccessible by public transit. Arguably, the most infamous example of the latter was

Jones Beach, the Long Island populist showpiece of Robert Moses, who, before its opening in 1929, built the underpasses on the approach parkways too low for buses, knowing full well that most African Americans did not own cars at the time.[18]

Even with a car, Black drivers had a host of obstacles to overcome once they rode out beyond the city limits. Gas stations and restaurants would not serve them or allow their use of restrooms. Hospitals would not admit them. Motels and boardinghouses had empty rooms but no vacancies, and "sundown towns" enforced whites-only rules after dark, on pain of persecution and violence.[19] While these exclusions were much greater in the South, they were widespread in the North until well into the 1960s and 1970s. As historian Gretchen Sorin notes, in *Driving While Black*, the road may have been public, but the roadsides were private and bristled with humiliation and danger for non-white motorists passing through and looking for services.[20]

Nor were the roads themselves free of prejudice, either from racist white motorists, bent on hijacking Black drivers for a lynching, or from police, who were learning to perfect the use of traffic stop as an instrument for harassment and worse. Versions of "the talk"—a traditional conversation that Black parents have with their children to educate them about how to evade white bias and violence—now included rules about how to behave when pulled over by cops on the road. These evolved over time from elementary advice, such as pulling over your vehicle immediately and responding politely and graciously to officers, to more direct instructions, such as keeping hands on the wheel and not reaching for any items without clearly informing officers.[21]

African American travelers found workarounds for many of these initial barriers. *The Green Book* (first published in 1936 by Victor Hugo Green as *The Negro Motorist Green Book*), which included listings for restaurants, hotels, vacation destinations, barber shops, gas stations, and more, directed Black travelers to businesses where they would not be subject to discrimination and white violence. Spacious cars, with large trunks, were specifically chosen for purposes of sleeping and food storage to avoid the indignity of being barred from lodgings and eateries en route to destinations. For this reason, Sorin records that the roomy Buicks (also considered more reliable and less likely to break down on the road) were the number one car choice of African Americans. So, too, fast cars like the Oldsmobile Rocket 88 were favored (by the NAACP's field director Medgar Evers, for example) for their capacity to speed away from trouble.[22] Other considerations included a legacy of loyalty to Ford brands because of the company's openness to hiring a Black factory workforce, though initially that was due to Henry Ford's belief they would be less militant than socialist-influenced white immigrant workers.

For the upwardly mobile, status was a strong factor in customer choice. In households with limited resources, the suggestion of wealth had even more appeal than with their white counterparts. Denied access to mortgages and suburban homes to fill with furniture, African American families could also devote a larger share of their income to cars. However, the mere prospect of Black people driving upmarket cars fueled no end of white resentment, spawning insidious anecdotes about the Cadillac-lined streets of inner-city neighborhoods.[23] In fact, after the war ended and consumption spiked, Cadillacs were still near the bottom of the list of brands favored by African Americans.[24] Regardless, the folklore continued to be a potent source of revanchism, reaching an apotheosis in Ronald Reagan's caricature of the Cadillac-owning "welfare queen," which helped him win the White House and carry forward his administration's cuts in social services.

Brown Mobility

African American drivers were not the only racialized population to encounter such obstacles in their travels. Jews were also barred from many hotels and restaurants, whether through explicit house rules or informal custom, and from more clubby properties, through covenants or "gentlemen's agreements." In Southern California, the spiritual capital of car culture, white supremacy on the road was enforced through a range of restrictions on the mobility of Japanese (through the passage of bicycle ordinances) and Chinese residents (through ID registration laws).[25] As Mexicans became the dominant labor force in the citrus belt economy, they acquired cars at a faster rate than the general population.[26] Controls over their ability to travel freely to perform agricultural work were more and more reinforced by fantasies about the region's Anglo settler past.

In *Collision at the Crossroads*, Genevieve Carpio illustrates the perpetuation of this fantasy by analyzing the official iconography of a Route 66 heritage festival that strove to present a whitewashed identity for the storied thoroughfare. Celebrations like this festival showcase nostalgia for Anglo cruising in vintage tailfin rides, hot rods, dragsters, and muscle cars while seeking to erase the multiracial past and present of the region through bans on Latinx lowriders, arguably its preeminent custom car tradition.[27] According to Carpio, this exclusion is the latest effort in a long history. Joyriding Chicano/a youth were criminalized as juvenile delinquents, and seasonal agricultural workers confronted a variety of obstacles on the road, including "sobriety checkpoints" that yielded few DUI violations but were utilized as sweeps for undocumented immigrants. Meanwhile, the impoverished Anglo migrants fleeing the Dust Bowl in their 1930s jalopies were championed as modern "pioneers," while the Spanish-speaking migrants who would form the backbone of the growers' economy were profiled as a public burden and were not accorded the right to travel freely.

The most toxic version of driving while brown occurred during the reign of anti-immigrant terror presided over by Joe Arpaio, the sheriff of Arizona's Maricopa County from 1992 to 2017. During his years in office, racial profiling was widely used in police traffic stops as part of his dogged, and illegal, efforts to detain and deport undocumented immigrants.[28] These efforts kicked into high gear in 2007 after his office entered into an agreement with ICE, pursuant to section 287(g) of the Immigration and Nationality Act, which granted his officers authority to enforce federal immigration law. These 287(g) powers were only supposed to be used if and after deputies had made a legitimate stop according to state law, but Arpaio instructed his officers to act as if they had unconstrained authority. He instituted "saturation patrols," through which traffic enforcement was specifically used to detect undocumented individuals. The patrols continued even after ICE revoked its agreement with Arpaio.

Arpaio stepped up his tactics after the 2010 passage of SB 1070, a state law that, among other extreme measures, required law enforcement officers to determine an individual's immigration status during a lawful contact if there is a reasonable suspicion that the person is undocumented. To beef up implementation of the law, which essentially obligated police to deputize as immigration officers, he drew on Arizona's tradition of civilian posses. These are comprised of roving vigilantes—Arpaio deployed as many as three thousand during his years in office—authorized to wear sheriff's uniforms, bear arms, and drive marked cars. The volunteers participated in his department's immigration sweeps and saturation patrols (or "wolf packs") that selectively targeted Latinx neighborhoods, commuter routes, and day laborer rendezvous points. Those apprehended faced a grisly term of detention in one of his notorious tent jails before deportation. After a damning federal investigation, a DOJ expert concluded that "Arpaio oversaw the worst pattern of racial profiling by a law enforcement agency in U.S. history" (which is saying a lot).[29]

In the wake of SB 1070's passage, many states including Alabama, Georgia, South Carolina, Utah, and Indiana passed copycat legislation. Other DOJ investigations in Connecticut and North Carolina found a similar pattern of disproportionately targeted Latinx drivers.[30] County sheriffs who ran on a nativist platform flocked to embrace 287(g), in order to empower their deputies with immigration law enforcement. Some of these powers, in Arizona and elsewhere, were curtailed by courts in 2012. But pressure from the federal government on local authorities to do the work of ICE agents was reapplied during the Trump administration in response to the growth of sanctuary cities that took a stand against such agreements to participate in the business of deportation.

In Arpaio's backyard, a vigorous coalition of young Latinx activists organized successfully against his abuses, ousting him from office and eventually turning the county blue in the presidential election of 2020.[31] But the *cultural* resistance to driving while brown began much earlier and, on the automotive landscape at least, flourished in the rituals and practices of lowriding from the early 1940s, originating in the Bay Area and spreading all the way to San Antonio. Drawing on the flamboyant spirit of the earlier *pachuco/a* dandy subculture, lowrider cars, with their dropped chassis, hydraulic suspension, and lacquered paint jobs, were a defiant show of Chicano/a barrio identity in the face of Anglo efforts to bury the Mexican heritage of the Southwest. Aside from their exceptional contribution to popular art and community pride, the lowriders openly challenged police power on the streets through their slow parades of dipping and bouncing vehicles. The convulsive movements of these audaciously decorated caravans (*la onda bajita*, or "low wave") were an affront to blue rule over the roads. Efforts at criminalization followed, in the form of tickets, warrants, and strict no-cruising ordinances, as the police and riders played cat and mouse all over town.

Police scrutiny and repression stepped up when lowriding was publicly embraced by hip-hop tastemakers and enthusiasts in the late 1980s and '90s.[32] The prominence of lowrider cars—especially the modified versions of the 1964 Chevy Impala in West Coast rap lyrics and music videos—turned the vehicles into folk icons at the same time as they attracted daily police profiling as gangbanger cars. Gangsta jams pumped out from the convertibles were also more of a provocation to guardians of sonic law and order than the old-school harmony soul favored by traditional lowriders. In cold climate cities, where open-air cruising was less practical, a burgeoning subculture of amped-up audio systems with formidable subwoofers ensured that beats would travel far beyond the cars of hip-hop aficionados.

The visually arresting uptake of lowriding in Black culture was a significant development but hardly novel when set within a long and rich history of African American car customization that included its own lowrider innovations. This passion for "aftermarket" modifications attained peak publicity in the pimpmobile conversions featured in 1970s blaxploitation and other mainstream films. Several of our interviewees recalled their gratification at owning such cars before they were incarcerated. Kevin, who spoke to us from his home in Indiana, reminisced about his "purple Cadillac, candy paint, gold metal flakes—everything. It was beautiful." More generally, Black popular music—from country blues classics like Robert Johnson's "Terraplane Blues" (1936) to Jackie Brenston and Ike Turner's "Rocket 88" (a 1951 ode that Sam Phillips called the birth of rock and roll) to hip-hop staples like the Lost Boyz's homage rap, "Jeeps, Lex Coups, Bimaz & Benz" (1995)—is a treasure trove of eroticized tributes to the mobile arts of stunting and cruising. Few are as puckish and plaintive as Chuck Berry's iconic "No Particular Place to Go":

> Ridin' along in my automobile
> My baby beside me at the wheel
> I stole a kiss at the turn of a mile
> My curiosity runnin' wild
> Cruisin' and playin' the radio
> With no particular place to go

While Berry, a convicted car thief, penned several roadster classics (including "Maybellene," "Jaguar and Thunderbird," and "Nadine"), 1964's "No Particular Place to Go" captured the blithe essence of driving for its own sake, without a destination in mind. But his 1955 song "No Money Down" was even more evocative of the immediate gratification, and easy credit, on offer from the postwar auto industry. Desperate to replace his "broken down, raggedy Ford" with "a yellow convertible four door de Ville" with "a jet off-take" a set of "railroad air horns" and a "full Murphy bed" in the back seat, the song's protagonist pulls into a Cadillac dealership with a "no money down" sign. The dealer is eager to deliver his fantasy: "Trade in your Ford / And I'll put you in a car / That'll eat up the road / Just tell me what you want / And then sign on that line / And I'll have it brought down to you / In an hour's time."

The transformation of cars into cool commodities is the leading edge of what sociologist Paul Gilroy calls "the enigma of African American auto-consumerism." In his influential article "Driving While Black" he considers how material deprivation and the allure of conspicuous tokens of wealth have led to an "overinvestment in automobility" on the part of Black Americans, while noting the equally strong appeal of the Black freedom narrative as imagined and activated through mobility by any means, including the Underground Railroad. He is skeptical about the resulting Faustian pact with consumer culture, especially when it involves an expensive asset like a car that loses its economic and status value rapidly. On balance, Gilroy finds that the value of freedom routes opened through Black car use is outweighed by the corrosive costs of devotion to a private good that functions as "an index of hegemony" in capitalist society. Dismayed by the glorification of luxury cars—Maybachs, Bentleys, Lamborghinis—on the part of the Jay-Z generation, he finds sustenance in William DeVaughn's "Be Thankful for What You Got," one of the few soul anthems with an anti-consumer car message.[33]

> Though you may not drive a great big Cadillac
> Gangsta whitewalls
> TV antennas in the back
> You may not have a car at all
> But remember, brothers and sisters
> You can still stand tall
> Just be thankful for what you got

Mobile Carcerality

Curiously, Gilroy's article does not dwell on drivers' fear of police surveillance and violence. Yet these threats were a real component of driving while Black from an early point in time. Private automobile use by Black Americans was of direct concern to a carceral state that had evolved from slavery's institutional control over the movement of Black bodies and was trying to contain African Americans within urban ghettos, the segregated school system, and other spaces of social confinement. After the gains of the civil rights movement, some things would only get worse. However surveilled and harassed they had been on the road for most of the preceding decades of the twentieth century, the chances of ending up in detention from police traffic encounters increased dramatically when the era of mass incarceration kicked in. As one of our interviewees put it, "The car actually became a way for police authorities to violate human rights."

There are many explanations for the doubling of the prison population from 1980 to 1988—the years of Ronald Reagan's presidency—and its continued rise in the decades that followed. The advent of "law and order" politics, the War on Drugs, the War on Crime, over-policing, neoconservatism of the New Right, the "liberal retreat from race," mandatory minimum sentencing, the explosive growth in the number of federal laws and regulations, and the doctrine of "broken windows" are among the factors typically noted.[34] Less commonly cited, but just as persuasive, are the consequences of inner-city unemployment from deindustrialization and urban disinvestment. African American workers were disproportionately impacted by the flight of industrial capital, and their communities were weakened by the shrinkage of public services in the austerity policies that followed the fiscal crises of the mid-1970s. Car manufacturers that had employed relatively well-paid Black employees for decades took a big hit from the oil embargo and fuel-efficient imports. Those workers were the first to be cut through the automation of lower-skilled tasks. Just like today, their jobs are the ones most threatened by autonomous vehicle technology: no group relies more on driving occupations (buses, trucks, and chauffeurs) for work than African Americans.[35]

After the factories were shuttered, members of this surplus labor pool were no longer needed. Their ability to move on or retrain was limited, and, in the aftermath of Black Power, their social agitation became increasingly militant. Jails and prisons were the carceral state's "warehousing" solution for large numbers of unemployed, and potentially subversive, inner-city residents who had few alternatives but to derive income from informal, or illegal, economic activity. The punishment for misdemeanors and petty crime was upgraded in order to fill jails, and the range of violations designated as felonies was expanded to match the growth of penitentiaries at the heart of what became known as the prison-industrial complex.

Following in the lineage of postbellum convict leasing, corporations quickly saw an opportunity to take advantage of their cheap labor when this population was put behind bars. Expendable on the outside, they could be put to profitable use while in prison either as workers or as consumers of costly services, such as phone fees, health care premiums, or jacked-up commissary prices. In states where private prisons flourish, those incarcerated are also billed for room and board.[36] Penal labor in the United States is explicitly authorized by the Thirteenth Amendment of the U.S. Constitution: "Neither slavery nor involuntary servitude, except as a punishment for crime whereof the party shall have been duly convicted, shall exist within the United States, or any place subject to their jurisdiction." But under conditions of incarceration, the line between optional and involuntary gets blurred, and the penalties for refusing to work are severe enough to warrant the description of forced labor. The range of goods produced in prisons at hourly rates as low as twelve cents includes car parts and automobile license plates.[37] Retrofitting and upfitting police cruisers are among the many services offered by UNICOR, the federally owned corporation that runs prison labor programs.[38]

Henry Ford's 1914 offer to pay his employees five dollars a day, twice the prevailing wage at the time, paved the way for the modern American consumer economy by ensuring that his workers had the disposable income to buy commodity goods, including the cars they were making. After the U.S. median working wage stopped rising in the 1970s, these goods had to be made more cheaply to fall within the purchasing reach of households. They could be manufactured overseas or in American prisons, where employers pursue a form of "in-sourcing" to compete with offshore labor, even with incarcerated persons in detention facilities located in other countries. This cheap, captive labor pool had to be created and renewed, and cars would play a central role in guaranteeing its supply when the policing dragnet over traffic stops and searches was recruited in the War on Drugs.

Police Mobility

Police on wheels were more than a step up from traditional beat officers on foot. Access to motor vehicles like Ford's Model B (from 1932), whose flathead V8 gave an edge in the chase, and accessories like the two-way car radio (from 1933), dramatically boosted the ability of law enforcement officers to control public space and surveil anyone in motion on the roads. Over time, encounters with police through traffic stops became the public's primary form of interaction with law enforcement officers, and in ways that have had far-reaching consequences for civic freedoms. For racial minorities especially, the promotion of the automobile as the shiny paragon of American freedom was soon at odds with the evidence of punitive overreach when it came to the enforcement of traffic rules.[39]

As the population of drivers exploded, police forces initially struggled to meet the challenges of ensuring road safety. This was especially true in the period of urban warfare over the right of way between plebeian pedestrians and gentry behind the wheel. The steep rise in traffic fatalities prompted the assembly of vigilante committees and citizen watches to promote traffic education and report on public safety violations. In order to resolve the class strife and to roll back the death rate, an extensive system of traffic rules had to be introduced.[40] As early as 1903, New Yorker William Eno penned a booklet called *Rules of the Road* that made the case for stop signs, pedestrian crosswalks, and other common-sense rules. But it took until 1930 to establish a more systematic set of regulations. Implementing these rules was another matter, however, since most drivers routinely violated them, and still do. The urgent need for adequate traffic enforcement was the number one factor in the rapid growth of police departments. This expansion occurred because deputies were now monitoring traffic violators who were otherwise law-abiding—in other words, virtually everyone. Compared to chasing robbers and gangsters, traffic duty was considered mundane. Compensation for its unpopularity among officers came in the form of broader powers over civilians, and this increase in discretionary authority inevitably led to the abridgment of civil liberties and racial profiling.

At the outset, it was not clear that deputies had the right to pull over drivers suspected of traffic violations. Sarah Seo begins her invaluable book *Policing the Open Road* by focusing on a 1918 Arizona Supreme Court case (*Wiley v. State*) that censured officers who tried to apprehend the driver of a speeding car in a manner that "was more suggestive of a holdup by highwaymen than an arrest by peace officers." The court decided that the officers had "violated" the "personal liberty" of the driver, who "having committed no crime" was "entitled to proceed on their way without interruption or molestation." Aside from the details of the incident (which resulted in the police shooting of the driver's wife in the passenger seat), Seo notes that the court's ruling on the right of drivers to proceed on their way "necessarily included the corresponding right to decide for themselves whether officers had legal cause to stop them. If they decided that an officer did not, then they would have had the additional right to refuse to pull over."[41]

What a world of difference to the present day, when car owners automatically concede the right of officers to pull them over, and when many drivers of color fear the consequences, including being shot. In her legal history of the intervening decades, Seo shows how cars not only transformed policing tactics but also how our privacy rights have been decimated by granting officers broad, discretionary powers over drivers and passengers of vehicles. Much of that history revolves around interpretations of the Constitution's Fourth Amendment guarantee against unreasonable searches and seizures. Did officers need a warrant, as required by the Fourth Amendment, to stop and search a private car? And, if not, how was it legally practical to limit their powers to protect the liberties of those inside the car? Over time, the courts decided that because cars operated on roads in the public sphere, where warrants were unnecessary, police, in their investigations of suspected felonies, ought to have the power to search persons and car interiors that would otherwise be considered private. It was held that, for law-abiding citizens, the costs of abridging the "right to be let alone" were outweighed by the benefits of guaranteeing public safety and welfare. When it came to protecting individual liberties, the state would carve out a portentous exception for the business of stopping cars on mere suspicion of illegal activity.

The attainment of that judicial endorsement of police powers hinged on the question of what constituted a "reasonable" search. Deference to police judgements about the reasonableness of specific searches became a default standard, and, in the absence of dashboard camera tapes that are the subject of intense scrutiny today, courts and juries routinely deferred to the officers' testimony when Fourth Amendment cases were brought against them. Seo argues that the upshot of determining reasonableness was a thicket of "judicial rules, which became more numerous, more specific, and more complex," and were "procedural in the sense that they direct *how* the police should police, unlike substantive rights, which secure the right to be free from government, including police, intrusion."[42]

This distinction meant that those more likely to be stopped and searched—minorities and poor people—could only hope, if not expect, that officers would respect these rules. Clearly, this fragile confidence in due process was a far cry from the right to refuse to be pulled over, as envisaged in the 1918 *Wiley* ruling.[43]

Granting police forces broad oversight over traffic safety gave them an arbitrary power to monitor almost everyone, since car ownership and car use became mandatory for the U.S. majority. In principle, the fear inspired by seeing the flashing lights in our rearview mirrors is the emotional degree zero of the carceral state—who has not experienced this feeling of minimum dread? In reality, this optional authority over everyone has always been unevenly applied, and especially ever since Black car owners ventured out of their spatially confined neighborhoods. Anecdotal evidence of discrimination, harassment, and violence long preceded the collection of statistical evidence regarding bias in traffic stops. After all, there is an endless list of minor infringements for which police can pull over cars: changing lanes without signaling, cracks in windshields, dimmed lights, dark window tints, low tire pressure. But the racial identity of drivers has been a disproportionate factor in the decision to do so.

Stopping cars for a minor violation was one thing, but the courts were more and more inclined to give police power to search cars on the mere pretext of suspecting criminal activity. No bright line roster of rules could prevent officers from making such pretextual judgements in the line of duty, especially if their own safety was at risk, as police departments insisted, albeit with little evidence to back up the claim. Seo shows that while Supreme Court judges agonized over the intrusive nature of pretextual stops, in case after case involving the Fourth Amendment exception, they extended the scope of the search to eventually include everything inside a car, even the contents of its trunk. Defendants could still argue that a pretextual search was unreasonable, but the legal margin for doing so had narrowed and, in the case of unjust conduct, officers were shielded from personal accountability by the doctrine of qualified immunity.

During the War on Drugs, the traffic stop and search (the mobile equivalent of "stop and frisk") became the primary gateway to mass incarceration. Crime patrols relied routinely on minor driving offenses to uncover criminal evidence in hopes of turning a traffic stop into a felony arrest. The targeting of those who fit the racialized profile of "drug couriers" was rampant, with predictable results. But even when data surveys of traffic stops showed a clear racial bias, the courts showed little interest. The exemption provided by what Seo calls the "Automotive Fourth Amendment" did not permit legal consideration of such subjective discrimination and, in effect, allowed the abuse to be lawful. Challenging racial bias in pretextual stops and searches based on equal protection, she concludes, would be more effective than continuing to wrangle over the Fourth Amendment.[44]

Thanks to body and dashboard cameras, the visual evidence of racial bias in shootings during traffic stops is ever stronger. That evidence, supplemented by witness cell phone footage, has brought home, in gruesome detail, the abuses inherent in the policing of cars. The consequences of giving cops free rein to intercept cars in this manner have been literally fatal for too many drivers of color. In April 2021, a few days before a rare jury verdict of murder for a police officer in the George Floyd case, Daunte Wright, a twenty-year-old Black youth, was shot and killed during a traffic stop. The fatal incident was less than ten miles from the Minneapolis courthouse where Derek Chauvin was on trial for Floyd's murder. As the shootings continue, it is not clear how local governments can effectively regulate their police forces. Despite the unprecedented nationwide mobilization of citizens in the George Floyd/Black Lives Matter marches—at the height of the 2020 pandemic lockdown—the movement to defund or "abolish" the police has been stymied in city after city, reinforcing the harsh and unacceptable reality that police autonomy and police powers are near untouchable in almost every U.S. city and county.[45] Nor did the marches result in any reduction in the number of police killings. According to the research of Mapping Police Violence, the killing has proceeded at almost exactly the same pace as before 2020, and with Black people being killed at three times the rate of whites.[46]

This privilege is reflected in the menacing appearance of police vehicles themselves. Although the clearly marked police cruiser, as we know it, did not appear until the late 1930s, its development since then as a distinctively aggressive presence on streets and highways is the most visible demonstration of the intrusive character of the carceral state. The concentration of paramilitary-style vehicles in "high-crime" neighborhoods considered to be hot spots gives these communities the appearance of areas "under occupation." Far from providing reassurance about public safety, or their occupants' capacity for de-escalation, the vehicles are regarded as an intimidation at the very least, and at worst an instrument of conquest. Indeed, the rationale for their deployment as guardians of traffic safety is very weak. In New York City, neighborhoods designated as high poverty and subject to such over-policing suffered triple the rate of pedestrian fatalities as low poverty ones.[47]

Police fleets have also benefited from the 1033 Defense Department program, which has supplied law enforcement agencies with more than $7 billion of excess military equipment over the last two decades.[48] The matériel (acquired for the mere cost of shipping) ranges from tactical armored vehicles (including mine-resistant models) to grenade launchers, military-grade arsenals, predator drones, night-vision goggles, combat fatigues, and other gear. Images of deputies wearing this gear and accompanied by these fearsome vehicles in heavily armed confrontations with nonviolent protestors have reinforced the public impression that police present themselves more as combat soldiers than as public safety officers.[49]

The standard police cruiser today is outfitted in the manner of a high-tech combat unit, albeit one with an onboard credit card reader for immediate payment of fines. Back in the era when deputies were routinely outrun by drivers they were trying to apprehend, the installment of two-way radio communications allowed for backup to cut off the car being pursued. The embedded gadgetry of present-day patrol vehicles represents a quantum leap in communications and tactical power. Features include drone-equipped trunks, bumper-mounted GPS dart guns, automatic license plate readers, voice dictation technology, facial and biometric recognition, thermal imaging, augmented reality eyewear, smart holsters, ShotSpotter gunfire detectors, and advanced computers and software that allow instant access to law enforcement and other government databases. Robotic and semiautonomous vehicles are on the near horizon. From their driver's seat, law enforcement officers can learn virtually where anyone within range has been and what they have done to earn an entry in the information network that services the surveillance state.[50] The vehicles that host all these technologies bear names—like the Ford Interceptor class—that suggest a martial purpose, and are hardly a comfort to the public that police forces are pledged to protect and serve.

The highly militarized fleet of today's police departments, and their "strategic response" personnel units, are a far cry from the fledgling organizations that struggled to enforce newly introduced traffic rules. Their evolution into squadrons of "warrior cops" with a sinister presence at the heart of our communities and the surveillance state presents a paradox. It was enabled by sharp upgrades in police mobility and powers, but it was also prompted and provoked by democratic access to automobiles and the freedoms afforded by them.

Peer researchers Derick McCarthy (top) and José Diaz (bottom)
with their cars.

Chapter Two

Experiences—Freedom Dreams

One of the best things to do is two, three in the morning you get in your car and you just ride on the highway, and put on some nice soft music. It takes you some other place. It just takes you. It's like a euphoria.

—Keyan

I love driving. I missed driving so much when I was inside. Twenty years with no driving. And when I could drive anything I could in there, I did. The trash cart, the golf cart to run the kids back and forth between the Family Preservation Center and the ADM building. Loved driving that damn thing. It was one of those long golf carts, you know? The gators, when we were doing building trades and maintenance shit, running tools back and forth? Love that shit. Give me that, I will drive that. Anything I could drive, yeah.

—Renee

The American love affair with cars does not stop at the gates of the prison, any more than the profit economy does. In the parking lot of Wallkill, a three-story neo-Gothic, medium-high security men's prison in Ulster County that is part of New York's vast archipelago of state penitentiaries, a guard arrives for his shift in his new, white Ford F-150 truck, talk radio blaring, his lunch packed in a small soft-sided cooler on the seat next to him. The cab is jacked up high above the ground, which may prove handy in winter when he must drive some twenty-odd miles over country roads in the snow to get to work. He guides the truck into a parking space below the coils of razor wire near the front entrance, where his coworkers can admire it as they trickle out of the prison at the end of their shift. Heading through the security doors, metal detector, and a series of heavy locked doors, he reaches the inner labyrinth of the prison, a network of drab, cinder block hallways, rooms, and staircases, glowing under dim fluorescent light, where people live out their confinement.

Behind Bars

For most of the men incarcerated at Wallkill, it has been years since they last drove, yet cars are the subject of lively conversations. Some keep stacks of automobile and motorcycle magazines in their cells and pore over them to pass the time. For a fee, those using J-Pay, the state's new and highly profitable inmate tablet program, can listen to songs celebrating high status cars, from classics like Tupac's "Picture Me Rollin'" to Lloyd Banks's jam, "Beamer, Benz, or Bentley." For an additional fee, the same tablet will screen videos with long shots of gleaming automobiles, films packed with high-speed car chases, or shows about retooled vehicles.[1] Some men reminisce and brag about the make and model of car they drove before prison, and the women those cars attracted. Of course, car talk might be just talk. In our interviews, formerly incarcerated men often laughed as they recalled the presumed embellishments. Somehow, it seemed everyone in prison had owned and driven a Benz.

The prison system regularly moves incarcerated people around. Here's a fairly typical trajectory in New York State through which someone might have arrived at Wallkill where the new, white F-150 is parked outside: Upon their arrest in New York City, they were first sent to the Tombs in Lower Manhattan. From there, with little warning, they were shackled and bundled into a Department of Corrections bus headed to the Barge—the floating jail off Hunts Point in the Bronx—only to be later relocated to the massive and decrepit jail complex at Rikers Island. There they languished for up to nineteen months before being sentenced and moved to Sing Sing, located just up the Hudson River in a town accessible by commuter train from Grand Central Station. Family and friends could visit, for a while. But after two months, they were transferred again, this time to Auburn, way up in the Finger Lakes. Over the course of the next eight years, they were uprooted time after time, cycling through Shawangunk, Five Points, and Fishkill before landing at Wallkill, from where they would eventually be released.

Arriving at a new jail or prison, a person must find their place. Sometimes they are fortunate to find themselves reunited with a friend or relative. But often they are alone and starting over again. People size one another up in a world where everyone is wearing the same green jumpsuit, yet they must figure out who has status. They have to seek the respect of peers within a penal system designed to humiliate them. People take note of who has visitors, receives packages, and has money deposited in the account with which they can shop among the limited goods on offer in the prison commissary.

Jameel is a quietly charismatic Black man whom others often deferred to as a leader. He was in his early fifties when we spoke, and he told us about his own experience arriving at Five Points years earlier, where he came in "with just the basic necessities." He had been on Rikers Island for a full two years after his arrest, before being first sent to Downstate (in Fishkill) for six weeks, and to Sing Sing for another few weeks. Then he was shipped to Five Points. The whole prison was fitted out with double bunks, so Jameel had a cellmate, Hector, who had been at Five Points for a long time. Since he was an old hand, he could have offered advice to Jameel in getting situated. But Hector was mainly dismissive, until three or four weeks later when packages and money arrived and Jameel suddenly had a radio, a TV, and other things, plus people on the outside who would support him. Then, and only then, did Hector begin to open up.

Cars are part of "how you get to know who is who" inside a prison just as they signify who's who in the parking lot out front. The automobile industry has sold the American public on the use of cars to mark status for more than a century, but, as peer researcher Aiyuba Thomas emphasized to us, they take on an extra meaning for those enduring incarceration, indexing some of what has been lost. First, there is the primary, fundamental loss of mobility, in being caged, that defines the experience of incarceration. Even within the prison, movement is hyper-limited. A set of bells announce coordinated movement times when the halls echo with the sound of men lining up. But even that limited mobility can be withheld by the guards at any moment. Then there is also the profound loss of personal privacy in an institution where even the most intimate spaces and experiences are moni-tored, and where guards routinely enter cells and dump or destroy posses-sions with impunity. In addition to these losses, the deprivation of access to a car is a source of secondary economic punishments. Whether seized by the state or the creditor or let go by family who cannot afford to keep up the payments on vehicles (which in any case may be nearly obsolete by the time their owner returns), the dispossession of a car and its value is part of the welter of carceral harm.

The men and women with whom we spoke explained how, for those enduring confinement, cars quickly become objects of longing. Jason, a young white man from a small Indiana town, confessed that he thought about his car every day during his imprisonment. He had only driven it once before his arrest. "It was really sad. The whole time I was in there I would think about it, and be like 'Man, I lost that.'" Keyan, Jameel, and Eric, three African American men in their early fifties who knew one another as classmates in the NYU Prison Education Program, said that after a certain amount of time caged, they began to imagine what it would be like to regain car ownership. This visualization, which is marketed every-where in ads and TV shows, was reinforced by their captivity. "The car is something that's placed in front of your eyes at all times," as Eric put it.

People talk about it in the yard, they brag about cars in their past, and they dream about cars in their future.

In women's prisons there are fewer motorheads, and there is far less car talk. The women we spoke with told us they talked about home decor with their friends and dreamed of homes to decorate, but car fantasies surfaced nonetheless. One African American woman who had settled in Cleveland after her release had a recurring, and, to her, surprising, fantasy during her many years in a New York State prison about owning a Chevy Impala. Another Black woman, Renee, dreamed of driving while inside the Indiana State women's prison where she was kept—in the meantime, she made do with steering the trash cart around until freedom came.

Like Keyan, Jameel, and Eric, Renee underscored what such a fantasy might suggest. Cars signify "freedom," we were told again and again by our interviewees—be they Black, white, or Latinx, male or female—and, for many of them, the freedom to move and the freedom to own converged. Behind bars, cars became objects of desire that combined status, mobility, and privacy in the heady promise of liberty around which prison dreams were woven. When they daydreamed about owning a Lamborghini or a BMW or an Impala, they were imagining how to regain social respect, or repossess beauty, but above all they were dreaming of unfettered movement.

For sure, some people inflated their history of personal car ownership. Everyone knows that "what you had" and "what you wish you had" might diverge. Just as they recognize the broader American societal truth that wealth can be an illusion. But then again, poverty itself could also be an illusion, in the sense that it marginalizes valuable people. You can know yourself to be worth more than your assigned place in the pecking order, worthy of a nice car even if it is inaccessible, just as you can know yourself to be more than the sum of your carceral record.

Early on in our work, research team member José Diaz rightly insisted that we could not understand how cars functioned in the carceral world without knowing how heavily gendered they are. He drew our attention to social norms through which cars express certain forms of masculinity, including how they are used and imagined to attract women, an insight repeatedly affirmed in our interviews with men. Kevin, who had driven a head-turning purple Cadillac in his youth, laughed as he recounted how a nice car "helps in the romantic sense." We also learned that certain models, like the Mercedes C class or BMW 3 series, are feminized, seen as "women's cars" by men and women alike. Men avoided owning them, though they might take their wife's or girlfriend's car out for a spin.

A typical, but related, comment was that a car is like clothing, or an exoskeleton that "defines me as a person, or a part of me" to others. Some emphasized that they keep their cars meticulously clean, while others had acquired more than one car to manifest different elements of their personality. For sure, some people had overreached, donned clothing that didn't fit, or that they couldn't afford. Kevin, who had driven that purple Caddy with the gold flecks, was circumspect: "You can get caught up in the trophies when you're young," he observed, "and not thinking clear." Jokes about Bentleys parked in the projects popped up more than once. A seventeen-year-old driving a Ferrari was comical, like a modern-day King Midas, and people around him were just cringing, waiting for him to crash it. But it seems no one dreams about driving a Ford Focus.

After Prison

Racial capitalism plays a key role in American automobility as well as American carcerality. By that we mean that profit is extracted through the existence of racial hierarchy in both systems, and the potential for further profits reinforces that hierarchy. A nice car promises Black and brown drivers an aesthetic or experiential escape, however fleeting, from the structural realities of the American racial system. Yet car consumption offers a thin form of equality when it depends on political and economic arrangements that profit from and police this desire. Many of our interviewees were well aware of how status-purchasing and consumer longing were part of the same racialized economy responsible for the deep poverty of the Black and Latinx neighborhoods from which they came.

Eric, who lived in Harlem but grew up in Brooklyn, explained how this dynamic primed his peers to want nice, even luxury, cars. According to him, the hunger for a good-looking vehicle is partly rooted in the hardship experienced by so many people, of whatever race, who were raised in working poor neighborhoods: "We grew up from nothing, you know what I'm saying? Like we want just to have something . . . when I was younger, we tended to want the best things no matter what it was." Living with deprivation and precarity had loaded acts of consumption with a supercharged meaning. "Wanting the best things" was an expression of self-worth, and so much more.

Many of our interviewees could readily identify how banks and car dealerships and advertising agencies and others profited from a system meant to keep them in their lane while dreaming of more. Marlon and Laquan, both African American men in their mid-thirties, who had known each other in a New York state prison, discussed this at length in one conversation. They named how car dealers upsold, how they turned profits from default and repossession, and how advertising agencies, social media, and celebrity culture stoked their desire. But they also were haunted by the tenacity of cachet and its relationship to masculinity. "The status game is complicated," Marlon told us. Both inside and outside of prison, "the car you have as a man renders your stature in society . . . and a lot of times, a person like me will pay a whole check" for the prestige. Even so, he laughed at the absurdity of the predicament. "I'm cognizant of the stupidity and the ignorance of it, but still I can't get past having to pay for that. I have to. I have to pay for it. I'm conscious of it but I still pay a whole check for this damn car." Laquan followed up in agreement. "Like he said, we know the stupidity and we still do it. We still go out and try to get it . . . You don't want to feel like you're not capable of attaining this. So a lot of times, people subconsciously feel like, all right, this person has it so I don't want to feel less than him." Of course, just because a person can critique consumption-based status, or can name the system of profit animating it, does not mean they can easily escape it, as any Marxist with a subscription to *Dwell* magazine can tell you.

Outside the penitentiary, the status economy merges with the compulsory nature of American automobility. As people emerge from prison, they must reestablish a place for themselves in the world. Reentry is a minefield. It is hard for others to grasp how exhausting, and how difficult, this process is.[2] Trying to describe the sheer bureaucratic challenge of it is daunting. The carceral system strips people of their former status, and, at every turn, the job seeker and apartment hunter are reminded of what an impediment a felony record can be. The parole system is "infantilizing," as one man put it, subjecting clients, sometimes for years on end, to curfews and other restrictions on privacy and mobility. State-mandated restrictions on housing or the absence of supportive family can leave people stuck in shelters for years. Most of one's previous possessions are gone—discarded or obsolete. Children have grown and may be estranged. Parents have aged. Friends and relatives have died. Spouses and partners have waited or moved on. And then there is the ubiquitous danger of being drawn back into a life that could result in a return to prison.

Rebuilding a life is an arduous and fragile process. It helps to have supportive family: a cousin who pulls out three new cell phones and says "choose one"; an aunt who offers her couch or spare room; a girlfriend who will cosign a loan; a wife who has been keeping everything together. It helps to have a job, and it definitely helps to have a car. Laquan noticed how people at his job treated him differently once he traded in the old beater car for his newer-model truck. Marlon was not surprised that people "treat you differently based on what you have, rather than what's in your mind or what you can contribute." He wanted to trade in his Mercedes for a cheaper, more practical car. But he didn't. And though he and his wife agreed to only drive their Honda for long trips because it was cheaper to operate, when it came time to drive to North Carolina to see his family for the first time since he was incarcerated at age twenty, they took the Mercedes, so that his family could say, "Okay, he did a lot of time but look, he's trying to do something with himself." He was not the only one. Several people with whom we spoke had plans for taking a nice car they had acquired or rented on a post-carceral pilgrimage to their parental home.

Amy, a white woman in suburban Indianapolis, was conscious of how she wanted a car that would not embarrass her teenage daughter with whom she was now reconnecting after nearly a decade in a state prison. She was painfully aware of the stigma of incarceration and how it might wash over onto her child, and recognized how the status effect of a nicer-looking vehicle blunted or papered over the stigma. But a car, in this context, is also so much more than status. Amy explained how incarceration decimates a child's ability to rely on their parents. We found that many mothers and fathers, on reentry, would do anything to offer the kind of reliable support and presence their children had been denied. Having a dependable car, a vehicle that would not regularly break down and make the parent's presence unpredictable, was paramount.

A few of our peer researchers and interviewees live and work in neighborhoods of New York City that are well served by public transportation. At the time of our research, some of them did not own cars, though they had plans to eventually purchase one. In the meantime, they cited the steep price of gas and the challenge of parking as designating car ownership a luxury, one they did not prioritize for the time being. But after decades of gentrification, most people returning home cannot afford to live in these transit-accessible parts of the city even if they could find a landlord willing to rent to them. The majority of our interviewees lived farther afield within the New York metro area, where public transportation became thin, or else in Indiana (near Indianapolis or up in the Gary/East Chicago area)—a contrasting site we chose, in part because public transportation was extremely scarce and car ownership was a necessity there, as it is in most parts of the country.

Aside from the relief at getting out of prison, returnees usually find themselves disoriented, overstimulated, and stressed. Facing a mountain of bureaucracy and obligatory appointments at state agencies, and in their quest to find employment and housing, in contexts without adequate public transportation, the need for a car becomes especially pressing. Jamal, an African American man originally from a small city in upstate New York, recounted to us his release from a state facility. He arrived at his girlfriend's apartment in a New Jersey town pre-enrolled at the university and ready to begin classes. While still incarcerated, he had applied to complete his BA. The day after his return, he attended a job fair and found work. Jamal had been assigned to report to a parole office in the next city over—a location that would require two bus rides and many hours of travel. But fortunately for him, his parole officer, on hearing this, offered to come to his home. For the past three and a half years, this officer continued to stop by the house, rather than making him report at the distant parole office. Jamal realized how lucky he was, because lack of public transportation is not a viable excuse for missing a parole meeting. The bus to his parole office only runs three times a day. "So that could turn into an all-day project," he pointed out, "of going there early in the morning, and then having to wait for an actual bus back much later." He could have taken an Uber or Lyft, but, at more than forty dollars round trip, that would quickly become too costly.

Americans have witnessed how in disaster scenarios, from Hurricane Katrina to the California wildfires, a car can be a life raft. But this is also true for most people under quite ordinary circumstances. We heard of women who finally were able to extract themselves from abusive relationships once they had a car, and did not have to rely on a partner to drive them to mandatory parole or drug treatment appointments, much less to Walmart to buy diapers. Access to a car kept those same women from the nightly danger of the dark bus stop. A few of our interviewees were driving for a rideshare company to supplement their income. Another told us that during a period of housing insecurity he was able to store his possessions in his car to signal to the relatives with whom he crashed that his stay was temporary. This man also told us of a friend who lived in her car two nights a week, since her job as a home health aide did not afford her time to return to her own bed between jobs. Aiyuba Thomas, one of our peer researchers, emphasized how crucial a car is to American parenting, an insight that was affirmed in many of our interviews. Between work and school, he drove his elderly grandmother to her many medical appointments and ferried his son around town. One woman, who endured seven years in an Indiana prison far from her young children in another part of the state, was only able to visit her kids once in the first year of her release. Only when she purchased a car was she finally able to see them regularly.

A car also makes it easier to escape from the pressure for a moment. You can be by yourself, and maybe even get a rush of that freedom feeling . . .

Doing Time on the Outside

But the struggle to get free is fraught with anxiety at every turn. America's carceral geography is vast and tentacular, reaching far beyond the prison parking lot. Millions are hauled into the maw of the penitentiary, and millions more are drained in its shadow. Recent media attention to police violence and the widespread use of cell phone and body cameras to document fatal traffic encounters has increased public awareness of the potentially harmful consequences for Black and brown people when pulled over on the road. Our interviewees were fully aware of these cases, and often mentioned them. But they also pointed to the multitude of lesser, but nonetheless significant, risks presented by the pretextual police stop. Traffic tickets are costly. An arrest, however minor the reason, can lead to a loss of liberty, and a cascading loss of jobs, housing, and cars themselves.

A car is a paradoxical personal possession. It offers privacy and freedom while traveling on public roads and through public space, but it also harbors the potential trauma of being followed and punished. A nice-looking car leans into the paradox. It draws attention to the owner's supposed economic status and good taste, but it can also draw the scrutiny of the police, armed and powerful personnel in their own vehicles. And so formerly incarcerated people are very careful about the cars they choose. Some fancy car models were known as "drug dealer cars" and were to be avoided. Patrick, who was in his mid-forties, explained that, unlike in his youth, he was "wiser now" and had opted for a car that would not attract unwanted attention from the police. Even as a pedestrian on the sidewalk, he confessed that "if a police car passes me, I'm clean, I'm not doing anything illegal, but I still get that sense of nervousness, you know, anxiousness." The last thing he wanted was to amplify that sense of dread while driving.

A car can manifest its owner's distinct personality. Some women decorated their cars with eyelash decals over the headlights and fuzzy steering wheel covers; men invested in fancy rims. Others said they liked to add tints. But identification by the profile of your vehicle inevitably leads to a loss of privacy. Certain cars are well-known to the police and to neighbors, and so their owners can easily be tracked. In turn, many people can easily identify the undercover detectives who routinely patrol their neighborhood in the same unmarked car.

Police scrutiny is far from the only factor in deciding which car to purchase and drive. For example, tinted windows, which were very popular among our interviewees, are subject to all sorts of legal parameters that vary by state. They were reported to us as frequent excuses used by police in pretextual searches. But they are nonetheless sought out both because of their "coolness" and the privacy they afford to those inside the vehicle. Peer researcher Derick McCarthy explained that attention from police officers was a secondary concern. "I'd rather have tints on the car to stop the neighbors and people that you see daily versus the cops that you see once or twice a day. I might see my neighbor ten times a day, I might see a cop once."

A number of formerly incarcerated white women we spoke with were highly aware of how traffic policing targeted Black and brown drivers. They knew they were sheltered by their race and afforded some privacy in their car. But they also had learned from experience that any traffic incident could lead to the running of their license, which would immediately reveal their status as former convicted felons. They were one fender bender away from denigration, and worse. Yet, as they all emphasized, this was nothing compared to what their Black and brown peers had experienced.

From a young age, many Black and brown men from heavily policed neighborhoods learn that the car is a site of arbitrary police power. Their liberty could be interrupted out of nowhere and replaced by the feeling of being trapped, and criminalized. Peer researcher Derick McCarthy recalled the routine. When he was a teenager growing up in a neighborhood of Brooklyn designated by police as "high crime," the cops would routinely pull over cars in which he rode. No pretext would be given; he and fellow passengers would simply be ordered to step out of the car. The officers would sit the kids on the curb and rummage through the vehicle. One officer would stand by them with his hand on his gun, while the other searched through the car, then they'd be told to get back in. On one occasion, he reported that "they searched all of us, took our IDs, searched us, tossed my whole car, pulled out my seat, I didn't even know at the time my seat came out like that. But he pulled out my seat, came and said to all of us, 'Yo, y'all got warrants, get them checked out. All right, see y'all later.' Threw us back in the car, and we just—they was looking for guns I guess, or whatever, they ain't find it. They was like, 'Aight, we out.'"

As they age, these men come to understand that being in any car is a trade-off. To exercise the right to be mobile, they would need to put up with the carceral surveillance of the road. In a conversation with a peer researcher, Braydon put this compromise into perspective for us. Growing up in Hempstead, a racially diverse suburban town on Long Island, he had been pulled over multiple times while in a car for driving while Black. The first time it happened, he was a teenager in the back seat of a friend's car driving through a so-called "red zone"—a neighborhood that the police target for pretextual stops. "There was no reason for them to actually pull us over," he pointed out, "it just so happened that that's what they decided to do." The driver had not run a stop sign or failed to use a turn signal. Braydon explained that in his neighborhood the police often pulled cars over without a pretext, hoping that "by the luck of the draw" they might find something incriminating. On that occasion, the officers lucked out. Without offering a reason, they made the boys get out of the car, searched it and found some drugs, and hauled all three of them off to jail.

The second time, Braydon was driving his own car when he was pulled over, again with no reason given. But instead of asking for a license and registration, the officers told him to get out of the car. They dragged him over to their cruiser, pushed him spread-eagle against the hood, and searched him and his entire car. "They didn't ask for a driver's license," he recalled, "they didn't ask for a name or anything like that. And at this time, I was maybe seventeen years old at the time, you know? They didn't find anything. I wasn't doing anything illegal. I was literally just fresh out of high school, you know? So I was really just more focused on just working, trying to figure it out. But I wasn't doing anything illegal at the time. I was young." But then the officers just let him go. "I asked them what it was for, and they just told me to go on my way, and have a nice day."

The third time was scarier. Braydon was a passenger, and the police drew their guns. "Like they actually got right out of the car, and stayed by their car, and drew their guns and made us get out at gunpoint. And we had done nothing wrong. It was just four of us in a car. I guess they felt threatened because it was four of us, I don't know. But that's how they are in these red zone areas, you know? A lot of the police officers, they automatically feel threatened." The cops said that they fit the description of some robbery suspects and proceeded to question them about why they were driving around with so many people in a car.

In other words, by the time he was in his early twenties, Braydon had experienced many times how freedom and the threat of its loss mingled in the car. Police surveillance of cars was normal in his neighborhood, so ubiquitous that it could hardly be avoided; it was just something to be endured, like the weather. Driving invites the attention of police, while walking does not. In fact, if he wanted to risk police harassment, he knew he'd be better off simply walking to the store. But this doesn't mean he is giving up the car—which is a practical necessity in a town like Hempstead. As soon as he got his car on his return home from prison, life felt a lot easier. He could commute to work, and didn't have to wait for inconvenient trains or buses, or for others to catch a ride. But he went on to name the paradox. "I think the car gave me an advantage, but it also, at the same time, increased my contact with police." Indeed, in his first week of having that car, he was pulled over twice.

Given how often he had been stopped and harassed in his life, we asked Braydon if he ever thought of giving up driving so he wouldn't have to tangle with the law. Like most of our interviewees, he said that was out of the question. After doing time, he might be more uptight while driving, more conscious of making sure no one got into his car with any drugs or paraphernalia, but ceding the privilege of driving in response to the threat of carceral harassment was not an option. Lisa, an African American woman from Albany who spent over a decade in state prisons but had since resettled in Cleveland, was rightly adamant about why this was so.

> Having a vehicle should not make me a target for the police. If I wanted to ride around in a gold-plated Lamborghini, that's my business. My car should not be the reason you pull me over. If I run a stop sign, okay. If I hit somebody, okay. But don't pull me over just because I'm Black and I have a vehicle. That makes zero sense. And I'm not going to not have a vehicle

to avoid getting pulled over . . . it's like I'm not going to not wear a hoodie just because you might think I'm up to something. I'm not conforming to your idea of who I should be.

As a few of our interviewees reported, the police, however much they were feared, were not all cut from the same cloth. Many offered up stories of corruption, theft, or abuse by cops. But some also remembered helpful officers who came to their assistance after their car broke down or after an accident, and then there were others who had been reasonable and polite after pulling them over for speeding. La'Trice (a fifty-year-old Indianapolis woman whose bankruptcy we detail later) recalled how terrified she was as a Black woman to see flashing blue lights appear behind her car as she drove through a white rural town in Indiana. Though no longer on parole, she braced herself. Convinced she would be rearrested, she forewarned her sister, in the passenger seat, to prepare for the upsetting spectacle of seeing her being handcuffed and taken away. But the police officer could see her palpable fear and sought to reassure her. He let her go without a citation even after he ran her license and saw that she had a record. Several people with whom we spoke had relatives and/or friends who were police officers. Speaking about the recent spike in carjackings at gas stations in a Chicago neighborhood she frequented, one African American woman who was a community activist said she feared a carjacking much more than a police encounter. But, like everyone else, she was also highly skeptical of the effectiveness of local police in reducing violent crime, while also pointing out the problems of police corruption and police brutality.

We have already seen how meeting the conditions of parole can depend on access to a car. But in a cruel twist, for those on parole—a term of surveillance that can last for many years—driving takes on added risks. Any contact with police can be rendered a violation of the terms of parole. Several of our interviewees on parole discussed how hyperaware and anxious the mere sight of a police car makes them. Even after being home for years and rebuilding a life, a police encounter could send you back into the cage. As Marlon put it, "It doesn't matter if you did anything wrong or not. It's just having police contact. So every time you see them, your heart jumps—just seeing a police car." This ability to instill terror gave the cops an additional arbitrary power over parolees. Marlon, seeking a quiet spot with some privacy, wound up sitting in his parked car to conduct his Zoom interview with us. We quote him at length for how perfectly he described to us the double bind of liberty and danger that is the daily reality of driving while on parole:

> Just to see them and the possibility that all right, this person could harass me and just put it in a note that they was in contact, and I could be reincarcerated for nothing. Like, something that everybody else would just brush off and say ah, it's—excuse my language—this asshole police pulled me over and just harassed me. Now, in my situation, in my life, just that contact could be a reason for a violation of my parole conditions, so you have to be super conscious. You have to be hyper conscious of any interaction with them. And like when I drive, I can't really even listen to music like anybody else would or have a regular conversation, because I'm always worried about am I going to get pulled over for going nine miles over or ten miles over? You know, we all look for that freedom, and just to have the freedom to drive, but you still are in a restrictive space, because if you come in contact with anyone and they write something up that says you were speeding ten miles over . . . they could say all right, you going back to prison. It doesn't matter what you're doing, what kind of job you got, how good you've been doing since you've been home. You're going back. Or you've got to report every week or we're going to come see you every week. Whatever. It's nerve-wracking. It's nerve-wracking. But I still enjoy my freedom of driving. I do. . . .

Even after parole supervision ends, someone like Marlon has to be careful, not only about how and where they drive, but about who they choose to ride with. Eric, another Black male interviewee, recounted that there was a time in his life when he physically searched everyone before they got in his vehicle to make sure they were not carrying a gun. He knew that if the police pulled him over for some reason and a passenger threw their gun under the seat, he might wind up in prison. But he also pointed out that the risk cuts both ways. Passengers were also vulnerable. Eric had met "quite a few people in prison ... [who] just happened to be in the wrong car at the wrong time." Without a car, you may have to take a ride whenever you can get it. With a car you can decide who to let in and who to leave on the curb.

Our Black and Latinx male interviewees also spoke of the sixth sense they had developed to navigate the city and the highways, especially to avoid or to drive with caution through the heavily policed areas they called "red zones." Vincent Thompson, a peer researcher, became interested in how these red zones map onto an earlier era of urban redlining. He drew our attention to how the concentration of arrests in these neighborhoods tend to depress property values, perpetuating a racialized system of downward mobility.[3] Some drivers we spoke with went to great lengths to avoid them, carefully mapping out and adding time to their journeys. One man laughed nervously as he described the absurdity of having to drive "all the way around Brooklyn" on a short journey, simply to avoid the red zones. "Just getting pulled over there is traumatizing," he explained. "The heart starts beating, you don't know what's going to happen next. You going to get arrested. I don't even think about the ticket, it's just getting arrested." So they took precautions. Even outside of those neighborhoods, many men told us that riding "four deep"—in other words, with three or even two other men in the car—would automatically invite police attention. Driving with women or children would reduce the risk. One Black woman told a peer researcher that wearing a work uniform to drive is wise, "so [the police] know you're a productive citizen in the neighborhood."

Yet these expectations were just rules of thumb. Another African American woman was driving with a friend in her Honda through a racially diverse, upper-middle-class neighborhood on Long Island—definitely not a red zone—when she saw the flashing blue lights behind her and pulled over. It turned out she had a broken taillight. "The officer asked me, 'Hey, do you have anything in the car?' Then they made a little, I wouldn't say whisper, but they got soft like, 'Hey dude, have a little bit of weed?' Like making it seem probably it was okay for me to say I did, even though I wouldn't never lie about it." She replied as her parents had taught her to—honestly— and acknowledged that she had a small quantity of marijuana. The police proceeded to search the car, where they found that "little bit of weed."

But even though she was the driver and car owner, the officers were laser-focused on the Black man in the passenger seat. "They were just being really difficult with my passenger, who was a male, African American," she recalled. "They was being really aggressive with their questions. I feel like they should have been focusing on me." The officers asked for his name and identification, and before she knew it he had been aggressively pushed up against the car and arrested. Her passenger kept asking why, but no reason was given. She assumed it was his gender that made him the target and not her. "I think he was charged with [possession of a small amount of mari-juana], but really in all honesty it was mine. I just feel like because he was a male, he was Black, and he probably looked a little—what's that term? Suspicious. I don't know, he had a hoodie on . . . Even though I told them that the weed was mine. They asked me, 'Did I have anything in the car?' I'm the driver, I'm behind the wheel . . . but they still took him."

Pretextual stops are nothing if not arbitrary. Everyone recognized that, but also understood that police clearly have the power to conduct them. Vincent Thompson, a peer researcher, was arrested while driving through his own neighborhood. He saw the police officers on the corner—"Mind you, we looked each other in the eye"—and so he was extra cautious. But as he turned the corner, sure enough they pulled him over claiming that he had failed to signal and that his tire was low. But he did signal. "You really think I'm not going to put my signal on when they right behind me?" But this gave them the chance to run his license, to pull him out of the car, to claim they smelled marijuana, and to search his vehicle. Who would believe someone on parole if the police said they broke the law? Who would doubt the officer who claimed to smell marijuana even if no one had been smoking? Eight months back in prison, after the loss of his apartment and possessions, the loss of an internship and other professional opportunities, an entire academic year wasted. He came away from this experience determined to defend his rights in the future.

> I feel like—yeah, I feel like now I can say that. Now I got my rights and everything like that, I know all my rights, I got all the paperwork. There ain't no marijuana in my car. Nah, you ain't—I ain't consenting to nothing. No, I don't—that's the stance I'm taking now.

But on hearing Vincent say this, another peer researcher countered that any assertion of one's rights was tilting at windmills. "I feel like seeing that on TV, and I know you can say it, and I heard you can say it, but when it comes down to actually saying it, I'm probably going to be very nervous just saying that." But, he added, "I have seen white people do that [with impunity]." He assumed that if he denied the police the right to search his car it would simply escalate rather than end the encounter. "I know that they'll say, 'Okay, hold on, we're going to wait, K9s [police dogs] going to come.' They're going to do a lot of other tactics before they say, 'Okay, aight, see you later.'" Even as a passenger he said he would not feel comfortable challenging a police officer who asked for a license. "I wouldn't. I don't know, I just can't do that, man."

Revenue policing in action.

Chapter Three

Shaking Down the Traffic Debtor

Writing to a French acquaintance in November 1789, Benjamin Franklin famously reported that "our new Constitution is now established, everything seems to promise it will be durable; but, in this world, nothing is certain except death and taxes." Today, his pronouncement could well be updated to include traffic tickets, since almost everyone is guaranteed at least one in their lifetime. Aside from filing taxes each year, a fine for a traffic violation is, for the vast majority, the most common and unavoidable legal interaction they will have with the state, and it comes in the form of a punishment. Unlike death and taxes, it is far from a natural by-product of living in the USA. And, as it turns out, traffic fines have attracted a good deal of recent scrutiny under the very Constitution that Franklin hoped would be durable.

Two years after Franklin wrote that letter, the first ten amendments to the Constitution were ratified by the states as the Bill of Rights. Most of the legal attention to the Eighth Amendment has focused on its bar on "cruel and unusual punishments," such as torture, extreme forms of incarceration, or inhumane methods of execution. In embracing a long-established principle of English law—that punishment should fit the crime—Congress was seeking to protect citizens from the tyranny of government overreach. By contrast, and surprisingly, the Eighth Amendment's other prohibitions were overlooked until very recently: "Excessive bail shall not be required, nor excessive fines imposed, nor inflicted." Indeed, it took the Supreme Court more than two centuries to strike down a fine as excessive. In *United*

States v. Bajakajian (1998), the court ruled against an asset forfeiture by the federal government that was judged to be "grossly disproportional to the gravity of the defendant's offense." In *Timbs v. Indiana* (2019), a case involving vehicle forfeiture by Indiana state authorities to which one of our interviewees expressly directed us in conversation, the justices decided unanimously that the Excessive Fines Clause also applies to the states, thereby extending protection to individuals from being excessively fined by all levels of government.

Even though it provided little guidance as to what should be considered excessive, the *Timbs* ruling opened the door to all kinds of Eighth Amendment challenges, including the out-of-control practice of "revenue policing" on the part of municipal, county, and state authorities looking to generate income from traffic tickets, court fees, and asset forfeiture. Arguably, this extractive practice originated in the early years of motoring when towns on major routes set up speed traps to take advantage of those passing through. Artificially low speed limits and excessively high enforcement, often using sneaky methods, are the primary ingredients of these ambushes, and towns with well-known "ticket traps" acquire a bad reputation for the schemes through which they ensnare guiltless motorists. But these scattershot tactics have mushroomed in recent decades into a more systematic model for funding the general operating budgets of jurisdictions, large and small, with little or no discernable relationship to the policing of public safety. In effect, revenue policing has become a form of stealth, or back-door, taxation that is grossly regressive, especially since the fines, fees, and surcharges are set at flat rates, and so they take a heavier toll on low-income motorists.

As many as thirty European and Latin American countries have sliding-scale penalties or "day fines." Finland has been linking penalties to personal income since 1921, and it is not uncommon for wealthy drivers there to incur speeding fines for $50,000 or more, with the threat of imprisonment for those who do not pay up. Infamously, in 2002, an upper-level Nokia official was ordered to pay $103,600 for exceeding the speed limit by twenty-five kilometers per hour. The sum of this day fine equaled fourteen days of his disposable income. While the Finnish system applies the principle of proportionality to wealth in penalizing reckless drivers, the U.S. flat rate system effectively discriminates among them. Equality of treatment produces very unequal outcomes when the penalties are excessive and imposed regardless of the ability to pay.[1] A $200 ticket is a meaningless deterrent to a hedge fund manager from Greenwich, Connecticut, who is pulled over on their way to the golf club, but it could be a devastating blow to someone who mows the fairways at the same club. The latter will have their pay docked for being late to work and, if they cannot pay promptly due to limited cash flow, they will face cascading penalties. If they cannot take a day off work to make a court appearance, they risk a bench warrant and loss of their license for debt delinquency; ultimately, they may face detention or probation for ignoring a court date or driving without a license, which will generate even more fines, fees, and lost income. None of this will happen to the financial manager. As for the well-connected—diplomats, government officials, municipal fleet drivers, and police officers themselves—they are exempt from such fines in the first place.

In the *Timbs v. Indiana* majority opinion, Justice Ginsburg wrote that "exorbitant tolls undermine other constitutional liberties" and, in tracing the Excessive Fines Clause back to the Magna Carta, she argued that such penalties should not be "so large as to deprive [an offender] of his livelihood." Yet such an outcome can easily occur when mandatory surcharges, draconian late-payment penalties, and collection fees are added to the original citation, enlarging the debt well beyond the means of low-income households, or when failure to pay results in a calamitous license suspension, vehicle impoundment and forfeiture, and/or a jail sentence. Not surprisingly, some of our interviewees said they had encountered traffic debtors during their stays in county jails while awaiting sentencing. To act as an effective deterrent to dangerous drivers, a traffic fine must be significant enough for them to alter their future conduct. But, in the absence of a proportional judgment tied to financial hardship, it can be economically debilitating for those who cannot "pay to make it go away."

Nor, the court seemed to agree in *Timbs*, should fines, fees, and forfeitures be imposed for the sole purpose of raising revenue for the state. This habit became more common in the wake of the taxpayer revolts of the 1970s and '80s, which resulted in substantial declines in government revenue. States and counties were increasingly forced to shrink government operations like their criminal justice systems or to privatize their components by extracting more revenue from offenders. In effect, judges were now pressured to impose monetary sanctions not just to cover court costs but also to pay the salaries of court employees, including their own. Once the system was corrupted in this way, it was only a matter of time before local and state officials began to sweep "surplus" revenue from these sources to help fund other government functions. Politically unwilling to raise the money through progressive taxation, and further squeezed by the Great Recession, they extracted it from the populations least able to pay. Police were drafted as de facto debt collectors, while traffic courts and municipal ordinance courts more than earned their keep through their efficiency at speedily processing cases and levying fines and fees. Public safety, the ostensible mission of law enforcement and the traffic courts, faded away in the rearview mirror.

The potential consequences of this often-baroque corruption go far beyond the economic hardship arising from debt entrapment. For drivers of color who are in the wrong place at the wrong time, a simple traffic violation can easily result in the loss of civic freedom or of life itself. The cascade of cumulative fines and fees invariably leads to warrants, court appearances, and jail time.[2] But for too many, the sentence comes much earlier from a fatal encounter at a traffic stop. When Daunte Wright was killed days before the Derek Chauvin verdict, he had been pulled over by police for an expired registration tag on his car's license plate. He is only one in a very long list of Black drivers—Sandra Bland (failure to use a turn signal), Maurice Gordon (alleged speeding), Samuel DuBose (missing front license plate), and Philando Castile and Walter Scott (broken taillights) among them—whose violent deaths at the hands of police were set in motion by a minor traffic infraction. A 2021 *New York Times* investigation found that police officers are trained to expect a degree of mortal peril to their person from vehicle stops, and so they anticipate using deadly force. In many cases, deputies put themselves in jeopardy through their own actions (e.g., positioning themselves in front of fleeing vehicles), and then respond, with fatal consequences.[3]

Deportation awaits many other petty offenders. Roland Sylvain, a green-card holder from Haiti, picked up traffic tickets twenty years ago and now faces being sent back to a country he left when he was seven.[4] Donald Trump's changes in immigration law and expansion of ICE's powers propelled Sylvain into this nightmare, but his predicament is all too common. In 2019, as many as twenty thousand people who were deported by ICE had been convicted of a traffic-related offense, and that number does not include those whose deportations may have originated with a traffic stop that revealed some lack of documentation on the driver's part.[5]

The Supreme Court rulings on the proportionality principle behind the Excessive Fines Clause addressed the original fine or forfeiture but have not extended to surcharges or administrative fees added on to the penalty.[6] In other words, they have not placed much of a check on the chain reaction that leads to these much greater, life-altering repercussions. If the *Timbs* ruling is more effectively cited to preempt states and counties from sweeps of fine and fee income to finance their general operations, then that may remove some of the incentive for excessive enforcement and criminalization of minor traffic infractions. But the opportunities afforded by policing traffic for racial surveillance and control will not be diminished, nor will the disproportionate punishment of poor people from flat-rate fines and disregard of defendants' ability to pay.

In this chapter, we take a different approach to the problem by considering traffic fines and fees as a form of debt owed to the state. These financial obligations differ from other forms of government debt because they do not derive from loans of the kind issued to students and businesses. Regardless, these fines and fees are treated as obligations that must always be repaid, interest accrues for late payments, and nonpayment is punished through a series of ever harsher penalties. Like most federal student loans, they are not dischargeable through Chapter 7 bankruptcy, and they can be garnished from wages.

Traffic debt is unique in other respects. When police officers issue a ticket, they turn free citizens into debtors and, since they are armed and potentially dangerous, the cops are also performing the state's monopoly on violence. When that ticket is written, the state is acting as an enforcer, judge, punisher, debt collector, and creditor all at once. When surcharges are added, the state or local government is both an originator and a beneficiary of the financial obligations. These roles amount to a powerful combination of functions, and they oversee an activity—driving a car—that is all but mandatory in the U.S. The federal government's history of subsidizing oil, roads, highways, and single-family home mortgages (and its corresponding neglect of public alternatives) has guaranteed that the vast majority of the population will break the law at some point. The likelihood of receiving a fine for a parking or moving violation or for a deficit of car maintenance is close to 100 percent during a driver's lifetime. Traffic debt is an unavoidable component of auto-citizenship, but unlike a true citizenly right or benefit, or a putatively equitable form of taxation, it manifests as a disciplinary sanction.

Traffic debt is comparable to other forms of household debt in placing an uneven, and punitive, burden on low-income and minority populations. But unlike with most civil debts, inability to pay can have destructive consequences—a license suspension, or a misdemeanor which requires an appearance in criminal court and can lead to jail time. While it may be nominally legal, many civil rights advocates consider the existing system of traffic fines, property forfeitures, and fees to be unjust and racially loaded.[7] Given that traffic infractions are a near universal outcome of the state's auto-centric policymaking, we would also argue that these punitive procedures are morally wrong. The practice of "profiting from policing" is the most egregious symptom of malfeasance at its core. But federal highway safety grants, to the tune of several hundred million dollars a year, help to subsidize this racket, because they incentivize the issuance of ticket quotas simply to ensure grant compliance.[8]

We take no issue with the need to maintain safety on the roads but question the efficacy of the current system in which wealthy violators can keep on speeding with relative impunity, while impoverished motorists face jail time for inability to pay. If public safety is the paramount concern, then enforcement of serious code violations is better served by programs of community service than monetary sanctions that end up criminalizing poor people. We also believe that debt amnesties and restitution are fully justified, not just as relief for millions caught in the LFO (Legal Financial Obligations) trap but also as reparations for harms that have flowed from government policies.

Driving While Broke

Debtors' prisons, which notoriously incarcerated the poor for their inability to pay off debts, were abolished in the U.S. in 1833. By federal law, you cannot be jailed for defaulting on your debts. Yet, in state after state, the practice is alive and well, either through loopholes or outright judicial disregard for federal authority. LFO debtors routinely face arrest warrants and jail time for failing to pay, or through contempt of court judgments when they fail to show up for a hearing. If they are unable to pay their debts through no fault of their own and are still detained, the judgment is also in violation of the Equal Protection Clause of the Fourteenth Amendment.

In case after case, the Supreme Court has upheld the principle that imprisoning someone merely because of their poverty is fundamentally unfair. Yet many judges in local courts pay no heed to this rule. While these unfair judgments can and do occur in the domain of civil debts, they are much more likely to occur in the case of LFOs, which are non-dischargeable debts owed to the state.

One of those Supreme Court decisions that referenced the Equal Protection Clause was *Bearden v. Georgia* (1983), which ruled against that state's revocation of the petitioner's probation and detained him for nonpayment of fines.[9] Judges frequently offer probation as an alternative to a longer jail sentence or imprisonment, typically *after* they have imposed fines and fees on an offender. In more than a thousand courts across the country, those who are too poor to pay their fines immediately are placed on probation under the supervision of private, for-profit companies that levy large monthly surcharges on top of the payments. Under this "offender-funded" model of privatized probation, debtors convicted of misdemeanors are ruthlessly extorted and face jail time when they cannot pay.[10]

The official justification for this form of outsourcing to a private entity is that the public is spared the cost of supervising the probation and detaining individuals for low-level offenses such as traffic violations. In reality, private probation supervisors in many states are rogue operators who act as debt collection agents, providing the muscle to shake down offenders for the fines and fees owed to the court.[11] For those unable to pay promptly, a judge will order the probation to be paid in installments, and often for as long as they remain in debt. The companies are contracted as a collection tool for these payments, while they profit from the monthly supervision fees. As a result, they have a vested interest not only in the court's ability to order probationary terms, but also in prolonging their duration. There are two key components of this lucrative racket. The first depends on the poverty of offenders, who are disproportionately Black and brown. Those who cannot pay are further squeezed for revenue, and often end up paying much more in supervision fees than for the original fines. The second is the threat of detention for "delinquent" probationers.

Getting ticketed for a minor traffic infraction would appear to be an unlikely pathway to arrest and detention. Yet the more aggressive generation and collection of legal debts on the part of states and local governments has resulted in the creeping conversion of traffic violations into potentially detainable offenses. In some states, like Georgia, Alabama, and South Carolina, most traffic violations are automatically considered misdemeanors, punishable by jail time. In others, extreme speeding and repeat offenses can result in direct judgements of arrest and detention; in Ohio, for example, a third speeding violation within a year carries up to thirty days in jail. Disobeying an order to appear before a court can generate the same outcome. In loosely regulated traffic courts and municipal ordinance courts across the country, judges threaten or issue jail sentences for unpaid fines, and for poor people it is easy to end up in that predicament.

How exactly does that happen? If an initial flat fine for a parking or moving violation is not paid immediately, it is likely to be beefed up by a mandatory surcharge, followed by late penalties, interest on the unpaid debt, and collection fees—ballooning into a sum far beyond the reach of those already straining to make ends meet. A license suspension for the unpaid debt will go unheeded by most of those who have no access to public transit, and who need to drive to work. A warrant and court summons will follow, and failure to appear can result in detention. Adding to the fiscal burden, judges, at their discretion, may impose a dizzying array of fines and fees for court and booking fees. In her research on sentencing data and legal documents in Washington State, Alexes Harris found that judges imposed these monetary sanctions according to a variety of moral—and therefore entirely subjective or arbitrary—criteria.[12] Coming up with money bail can be a huge financial obstacle, and if they are handed a jail sentence, offenders in many jurisdictions will also be charged for room and board ("pay-to-stay") while in detention.

On release, all the aggregate debt is still owed and may have accumulated more through interest and additional surcharges. The challenge of digging out of the post-carceral debt trap is colossal for those struggling to find employment and housing.[13] In *Who Pays: The True Cost of Incarceration*, a 2015 multistate survey of formerly incarcerated people and their families, researchers for the Ella Baker Center for Human Rights found that they owed an average of $13,607 for "court-related fines and fees" alone."[14] The outcome can literally be a lifetime of debt and therefore a perpetual relationship with the criminal justice system in which the "debt to society" is never fully paid off.

Confronted with this significant debt burden, even a relatively small post-carceral increment, like monthly parole supervision fees (for which some states charge two or three hundred dollars), can be a significant obstacle, prompting parolees into illegal activity, at the risk of resentencing, to pay them. Given the challenge of reinstating a driving license (indispensable in most parts of the U.S.), and the likelihood of stepped-up police surveillance for those with a criminal record, it is no surprise that further traffic violations often follow, resulting in reincarceration. The deadweight of LFOs deepens other challenges faced on reentry, including restricted access to public sector employment, public housing, social welfare programs, and voting rights. It is tragic to consider that this vicious cycle of discipline, impoverishment, detention, and lifelong debt service can be set in motion initially by something as minor as a parking ticket, and yet, in many jurisdictions, there is little to check the momentum.

Suspension of a driving license is a particularly harsh element of the cycle. In the auto-centric U.S., cutting off the lifeline of access to their cars has far-reaching consequences for the financial stability and well-being of a population under fiscal stress. Licenses can be revoked in some states for drug offenses unrelated to driving, but most suspensions are for outstanding traffic debt. While several states have recently passed reforms restricting this form of punishment, thirty-three states and Washington,

DC, still routinely suspend, revoke, or refuse to renew licenses, with a devastating impact on drivers' access to work, childcare, health care, and food. Forced to choose between meeting these basic needs and risking criminal charges by driving on a suspended license, many drivers (an estimated eleven million nationwide have had licenses revoked)[15] opt for the latter. Not surprisingly this predicament came up repeatedly in our interviews. In one group interview we held, a Long Island resident reported that driving with a suspended license was "regular" in his neighborhood. Another man from New York, offered confirmation: "Honestly, I would still drive. I would have to still drive. I don't want to [but I have to]." The high percentage who lose employment, or have to take lesser-paying jobs, after losing their driving privileges are even less able to pay up and reinstate their licenses. Nor does the threat of suspension or vehicle impoundment result in more efficient collections of penalties. If you cannot afford the initial fines, the likelihood of being able to pay off even greater debt is slim, especially if you are hit with a job loss as a result. Further financial ruin and incarceration are the more probable outcomes.

Going after petty offenders in this aggressive fashion is generally ineffectual as a law enforcement mechanism. In most instances, the connection between public safety and this extreme punishment for "driving while broke" is nonexistent, since even serious offenders would still be driving if they had paid their tickets. The ability to avoid further sanctions turns entirely on who can afford to pay. Free to Drive, the national coalition seeking to outlaw license suspensions, holds that such restricted privileges should not be deployed as a debt collection tool, or to punish poor motorists, but should be reserved solely for dangerous driving.[16] As for the court fines and fees that may result from further entanglement with the carceral system, studies show that the revenue generated from these penalties is often lower than the costs of collection, enforcement, and detention.[17]

In common with other classes of traffic debt, the impact of license suspensions is racially uneven. Driven by Justice, the statewide coalition that pushed for the reform of New York's laws, mapped the data onto zip codes and found that the suspension rates were much higher in poor and minority neighborhoods.[18] Back on the Road California completed a survey showing similar results for neighborhoods in the Bay Area and Los Angeles.[19] In Virginia, where African Americans are 22 percent of the population, they represented almost 50 percent of the drivers who had their licenses suspended.[20] A key element behind the national campaign to change these laws is the conclusive evidence that their implementation is fundamentally unfair.

Much of the energy behind these reform efforts was inspired by the landmark 2015 report by the Department of Justice on policing and collection practices in Ferguson, Missouri. The investigation was launched after Michael Brown, an unarmed Black teenager, was fatally shot by a white police officer in 2014, triggering a long summer of street confrontations that added fuel to the Black Lives Matter movement. The report found racial bias at all levels of the police department, from the everyday culture of its officer corps to the data showing uneven treatment in use of force, traffic stops, and ticket writing. These disparities were aggravated by the municipality's increasing reliance on policing and courts for budget revenue. In 2013, Ferguson issued three arrest warrants for every household. City officials exerted constant pressure on the police department and court staff to raise money from fines and court fees:

> In March 2010, for instance, the City Finance Director wrote to Chief Jackson that "unless ticket writing ramps up significantly before the end of the year, it will be hard to significantly raise collections next year. . . . Given that we are looking at a substantial sales tax shortfall, it's not an insignificant issue." Similarly, in March 2013, the Finance Director wrote to the City Manager: "Court fees are anticipated to rise about 7.5%. I did ask the Chief if he thought the PD could deliver a 10% increase. He indicated they could try."[21]

The push to increase the "productivity" of citation issuance was reflected in officer evaluations and promotions, and resulted in a chronic pattern of arbitrary and racially driven enforcement. Consequently, the residents of the city's predominantly African American neighborhoods were regarded "less as constituents to be protected than as potential offenders and sources of revenue."[22]

The Ferguson report blew the lid off the scandal of revenue policing, while the momentum of Black Lives Matter pushed into public consciousness the full extent of racially motivated abuse of their powers on the part of the nation's police forces. Scrutiny of the fiscal conduct of law enforcement and court systems in other states revealed that Ferguson was not an isolated, regional instance of citizen exploitation. A stinging report from the Lawyers Committee for Civil Rights was entitled *Not Just a Ferguson Problem— How Traffic Courts Drive Inequality in California,* and No Price on Justice, a New York reform coalition, produced its own version, called *New York's Ferguson Problem.*[23] One national study found that as many as thirty-four New York localities were just as reliant on fines and fees revenue in 2017–18 as Ferguson had been in the years before Brown was killed.[24] A comparable survey of three cities in Georgia conducted by the Institute for Justice found that they generated such a high level of revenue from fines, forfeitures, and fees as to warrant the description of "taxation by citation."[25]

The publicity generated by the Ferguson report also prompted some judges—concerned about the crumbling integrity of their professional authority—to speak out about the pressure to raise revenue to keep their own courts running.[26] The former chief judge of the New Orleans criminal court—where LFOs accounted for almost two-thirds of the general operating budget—acknowledged that it creates "an appearance of impropriety" when judges have to bring in their "fair share" of revenue in this way.[27] Distrust of police officers is already deeply rooted in low-income and minority communities. But the shredding of belief in the capacity of courts and legal officials to play fair strikes even harder at the legitimacy of the judicial system. The spectacle of judges preying upon the most vulnerable members of the general population to pay their salaries is not a good look, to put it mildly, for a society governed by the rule of law. Evidence of fees and surcharges being used for perks and personal expenses further erodes respect for the system; in one case in Louisiana, funds from fines and fees were spent on "luxury goods, including supplemental health insurance for judges, two Ford Expeditions, a leather upholstery upgrade for a take-home vehicle, and a full-time private chef."[28]

In a December 2017 ruling against these practices, Sarah Vance, a federal judge, referred to the "institutional incentive" followed by judges in the Orleans Parish court, and condemned the absence of any ability-to-pay inquiries in their judgements. In the wake of the Ferguson report, the Department of Justice took the rare, and bold, step of sending a letter to state court administrators warning them against operating courthouses as for-profit ventures.[29] The letter chastised judges for using arrest warrants as a way to collect debts, and reminded them that jailing indigent people for being unable to pay fines through no fault of their own violates the US Constitution.[30] However, the Supreme Court, going back to the *Bearden* ruling, has provided little guidance to judges in determining whether offenders are truly indigent or whether they are "willfully" refusing to pay fines, in which case, detention can apply. As a result, the discretionary nature of this determination allows court officers leeway to go on shaking down poor people in this way because they cannot replace the revenue that would surely be lost from properly implementing the law.

Neo-Feudalism?

This loss of credibility in the integrity of courts is by no means confined to the criminal justice sector. The general transfer of fiscal responsibility from the state to the individual, which we associate with neoliberalism, has eroded the probity of all public institutions that are now forced to depend on private funding or to extract more and more revenue from users. A single-minded focus on fundraising not only distorts their public mission but also undermines public faith in their capacity to provide services fairly. When the public sector is so strapped that it struggles to meet these expectations, it gets a bad reputation, and the vicious circle is complete.

The courts are hardly alone. Most publicly funded institutions are in a similar quandary. Public universities abandoned by state legislatures have had to rely more and more on tuition hikes to cover costs, with the predictable outcome of a steady rise in student debt. Resentment at being landed with a lifetime of student debt service is understandable, but it is misdirected when universities are themselves blamed for the predicament. The alternative for colleges is to turn to Wall Street for loans, with equally foreseeable results. Public universities are now saddled with several hundred billion dollars of institutional debt.

Cities have also been squeezed, and have racked up record amounts of municipal debt—total borrowing in 2020 rose to a whopping $3.9 trillion.[31] Having lost the political will, or the means, to raise revenue through progressive taxation, officials resort to the sordid business of squeezing their constituents in order to service muni bond loans underwritten by Goldman Sachs and other big investment banks. In turn, the fines and fees are pledged as collateral, to back the bond issues in the first place.[32] Impaired by policies that overwhelmingly tilt toward private transportation, public transit systems in particular have suffered from the funding crunch. New York's Metropolitan Transportation Authority had $49.2 billion of outstanding debt by July 2021 and, over the next year, was projected to be paying out more than a quarter of its annual budget in debt service.[33]

In lieu of proper funding for these public agencies, authorities resort to hiking user fees or, in the case of the criminal justice system, look to LFOs to fill the budget gaps. Either way, the burden falls unduly on lower-income populations. One glaring exception to the pattern of public defunding has been police departments, which despite declining crime levels have seen a significant increase in government support. From 1977 to 2018, state and local government expenditure on police increased nearly threefold, from

$43 billion to $119 billion, while spending on corrections showed an even greater increase.[34] Law-and-order conservatives today argue that Black Lives Matter has undermined public faith in the integrity of police conduct and that the movement to "defund the police" will result in a further loss of legitimacy. Yet this position must be seen in the context of a long-standing right-wing campaign of austerity to "starve the beast" of government while carving out an exemption for law enforcement spending. Indeed, in the wake of the George Floyd protests, some municipal police budgets were cut, but within a year most of these cuts were restored, and in many instances supplemented by increases.[35]

Reliance on traffic debt and other LFOs to help cover public budgets is a byproduct of such austerity policies, designed explicitly to shrink or privatize the public sector. But revenue policing also belongs to what economist Michel Hudson calls the "tollbooth economy," in which fees and rents are systematically extracted from users of vital utilities and services that used to be adequately funded public goods.[36] In this neo-feudal arrangement, the fees, extorted by would-be monopolists at chokepoints in the economy, are non-optional and the takings are predatory in nature. In critiquing the new "robber barons" of the digital era like Jeff Bezos, Bill Gates, and Mark Zuckerberg, Michael Lind reminds us that the original meaning of the term "referred to German aristocrats with castles along the Rhine who used the threat of violence to extort tolls from passing ships."[37] These monopolists of platform capitalism cash in on the threat of deprivation or blocked access to the digital highways, and they extract their tolls through the stealth tactics of data mining, i.e., the small print of "terms of service" that secures the consent of users to the commercial use of their personal data.

As the most conspicuous player in this neo-feudal economy, Big Tech has attracted criticism for its profiteering through abuse of proprietary power, and its resistance to fiscal regulation. But its extractive business models are not unique to private capital. They are echoed in similar efforts on the part of the auto-centric state, and are exemplified in the taking of income from petty code violations in order to finance general funds. Cops who oversee the real, and not the digital, highways have more discretion about who they will ticket and when to do it, and they carry the threat of violence on their person. A 2017–2018 study for *Governing* magazine found almost six hundred U.S. jurisdictions where fines and fees account for more than 10 percent of the general budget, and for almost half of these it was more than 20 percent. These localities tend to be concentrated in rural areas with high poverty rates and a limited tax base, and especially in Southern states like Arkansas, Georgia, Louisiana, Oklahoma, and Texas. Two townships in Louisiana drew more than 90 percent of their general revenue from traffic fines, forfeitures, and fees. And in Georgia, home to many infamous speed traps set for Disney-bound motorists, nearly all traffic violations are criminal misdemeanors, carrying fines of up to $1,000 and the threat of jail time.[38] The U.S. Commission on Civil Rights found that jurisdictions that rely heavily on revenue from fees and fines have a higher-than-average share of African American and Latinx residents.[39]

New York earned plaudits for its Driver's License Suspension Reform Act, signed by Governor Andrew Cuomo on New Year's Eve 2020. While the state thereby put an end to the practice of suspending a driver's license because someone cannot afford to pay a traffic fine, its regime of fines and fees is still one of the more punitive and predatory. In fact, it clocked in as sixth-worst offender in the *Governing* survey of revenue policing. New York has more than 1,300 town and village courts that are funded entirely by their localities and operate with little oversight from the state. These courts are presided over by 1,776 elected judges, though only 700 of them hold a law degree. Officials have a strong and unchecked incentive to harvest revenue from petty traffic violations to fund government budgets, and they rarely consider ability to pay when sentencing.[40] As much as 90 percent of court revenues in the state are generated through fines, fees, and surcharges on vehicle and traffic violations. The New York City Bar Association has called for a sweeping reform of mandatory court fees in noncriminal dispositions like traffic infractions.[41]

Not only has New York state failed to regulate these local courts, it also competes with them for a slice of the pie by adding surcharges to every traffic fine. Most of these surcharges start at $93 for a first-time offense in a town or village court and $88 for a city court, even when the fines themselves are for a lesser amount. These levies increase considerably through Public Safety Fees and Driver Responsibility Assessment Fees, starting from $300 for anyone with recent violations and six points or more on their driver record (or $750 in the case of an alcohol/drug-related infraction). If a driver's violations turn into a misdemeanor or felony, the mandatory surcharge is $175 and $300 respectively, in addition to fees imposed for crime victim assistance and DNA testing. Theoretically, the surcharge revenue goes into the state's "criminal justice improvement account," used for victim and witness assistance services, and to pay for court-appointed attorneys, but the legislature routinely sweeps these funds for other purposes, or to fill general budget gaps.[42]

Several years ago, the state tried to reduce the opportunity for drivers to enter into plea bargaining over their speeding violations. This practice, which had resulted in lost revenue for the state, allowed local courts to collect the fine as a parking violation, but saved the driver from the state surcharge being reported to the DMV for collection.[43] The governor's proposal—to add a new $80 surcharge on any such plea bargains—was rejected by the legislature, but was widely interpreted, at the time, as a naked money grab on the part of the state.

Such imbroglios are revealing of the grubby competition between state and local governments over revenue shares. But regardless of how the spoils are divided, neither jurisdiction takes into consideration the ability of violators to pay. New York law does not require courts to lower the amount of a fine when ticket recipients are too poor to pay and, since the "tough on crime" Sentencing Reform Act of 1995, it is legally impermissible to waive mandatory surcharges on the basis of evidence of financial hardship. For low-income or indigent debtors, there is no exit from the destructive cycle that begins with a minor violation and leads to arrest and detention for motorists who drive with suspended licenses. Before pressure mounted to change the law, 75 percent of those suspended continued to drive, risking criminal charges and prison sentences for doing so.[44]

Rentier States or Harm Reducers?

Nations that rely on external income from trading their natural resources are often called "rentier states." The oil states of the Middle East and North Africa are the best examples of societies in which these external rents are large enough to spare citizens from taxation. Internal rents take many forms, but they are primarily generated through government ownership of land or assets or through use of public authorities to issue levies. Obvious examples are leasing or mining fees collected for private use of public lands. Taxation itself is sometimes classified as rent-seeking behavior on the part of the state, and we would include revenue policing in that category since it involves the opportunistic application of government power. This widespread practice encroaches on the constitutional right not to be excessively fined and exhibits clear evidence of government profiteering off the public use of roads and highways.[45] All of the evidence suggests that the monetary sanctions are disproportionately imposed on racial minorities and low-income populations. When ticketing is combined with the bias of police profiling through pretextual searches, the rent-seeking looks more and more like a racially driven extortion racket.

The primary rationale for traffic citations, even when they are excessive or regressive in their flat application across all socioeconomic strata, is that they are legitimate and effective measures to protect individuals and communities from harm. Yet, when all the harmful impacts of rent-seeking are considered, it is more difficult to see how stepped-up police enforcement of often petty violations of traffic codes can be an overall contribution to public safety. And, in the wake of the racial reckoning that followed the killing of George Floyd, there is more public awareness of how policing in and of itself poses a direct threat to the safety and security of communities. As a result, efforts are now afoot to reduce or eliminate the role of armed police officers in traffic enforcement and seek out automated or community-based alternatives. Berkeley, the home of policing innovations in the early twentieth century, is the first municipality to prohibit police entirely from conducting traffic stops, and other cities like Portland, Minneapolis, and New York are likely to reorganize their duties in the same spirit of reducing police interactions with motorists.[46]

Resistance from police departments is guaranteed but it won't necessarily come from rank-and-file officers, who generally resent being assigned ticketing quotas or being promised overtime and pay raises as an incentive for writing additional tickets. Listen to Randy Petersen, a former police officer in Texas, recounting the futility of his career in traffic enforcement:

> During my twenty-one years as a police officer, I would conservatively estimate that I investigated over 1,000 traffic accidents. In all of those accidents, I never found an expired registration sticker to be the cause of the accident. I never found that a driver waiting to signal until 90 feet before a turn, instead of the required 100 feet, was the cause of an accident. I never found an air freshener dangling from a rearview mirror to be the cause of highway carnage . . . Much of the traffic code criminalizes things that do not contribute much to roadway safety, which is almost universally the reason given for their enforcement.

Petersen goes on to recall "management staff meetings . . . where the chief would express concern over a decline in citation productivity . . . of the patrol division or, on occasion, an individual officer, it was always clear that ticket-writing was a measure of an officer's productivity." Moreover, "the city board would inquire about any drop in ticket writing and it was made clear to the supervisors that this was unacceptable." As for traffic safety, it was "only tangential to the discussion."[47]

Ultimately, libertarians like Petersen (who now works for the policing initiative at the conservative Texas Public Policy Foundation) are troubled by the ineffectuality of traffic regulation, especially, as he points out, since "none of us are capable of complying with the entirety of the vehicle code for any length of time." Laws that criminalize the majority of the population on a daily basis are a prime example of an overregulating state, and so Petersen believes that officers who are ordered to enforce them simply to gin up revenue are breaking faith with what he calls the "conservative view of liberty."

A broader view of public safety would consider the full spectrum of harms generated by police involvement in traffic enforcement, ranging from the direct threat to roadway safety posed by a traffic stop on a busy highway to a car chase on a city street, to the catastrophic impact on community stability from incarcerating petty offenders who cannot pay fines. This results in permanent declines in income, loss of housing and opportunities like education and employment (not only for the incarcerated but their family members), bills for mental health support, loss of children sent to foster care or extended family, and, of course, the loss of life from use of deadly force at traffic stops.[48]

For many of those able to stave off detention, paying down their traffic and court debt is only possible by incurring other debts through payday loans and car title loans or through the illegal pursuit of income. As one of our interviewees put it, euphemistically referring to the pressure to raise the funds for traffic and carceral debt while working a minimum wage job, "Sometimes you gotta do what you gotta do to get money and then, you know, you have to pay these people to get them off your back." In one Alabama study of individual experiences with fines and fees, 44 percent of those surveyed sought out high-interest predatory loans, while 38 percent admitted to having committed at least one crime in order to pay off their legal debt: almost three in ten, with only traffic violations or misdemeanors as prior offenses, admitted to committing more serious crimes to service that debt. Almost two-thirds reported that they had to seek out money or food assistance from a faith-based charity or church because of the debt, and the vast majority gave up necessities like rent, medical bills, or child support in order to do so.[49] How is community security served by plunging so many into forced choices like these to pay off petty government debt? Only a very limited notion of public safety would exclude consideration of such ruinous consequences.

The intrusive entry of traffic police into areas profiled as "high crime" neighborhoods further eviscerates trust in law enforcement among communities with little reason, historically, to equate the presence of armed officers with safety. (In 1960, James Baldwin compared an officer "moving through Harlem" to "an occupying soldier in a bitterly hostile country.")[50] Under the "broken windows" theory of policing, which championed a crackdown on minor code violations, citations for traffic infractions like jaywalking were among the strategic measures chosen to deter lawlessness and reinforce moral and physical order in low-income neighborhoods. Broader applications of the broken-windows doctrine included highly controversial policing tactics like "stop-and-frisk" and pretextual traffic stops. Harsh criticism of these procedures has contributed to the Black Lives Matter call to transfer public funding away from heavily armed interactions to community-based enforcement that places a priority on public health. Many of the proposed alternatives appeal to data-driven evidence for their superior efficiency, but they are also informed by a growing consensus that structural racism itself is a deadly threat to public safety.

With 42,000 fatalities from motor vehicle collisions in 2020, roadway safety is not a trifling problem.[51] But historically, the largest contribution to injury prevention has come not from stricter code enforcement but from driver education, changes in road and automobile design, and campaigns like Mothers Against Drunk Driving (MADD). For example, the 1965 publication of Ralph Nader's *Unsafe at Any Speed* prompted regulations that compelled the big auto makers to reengineer their products to mitigate the "second collision" of human bodies with the interior of vehicles.[52] The impact of these design changes saved immeasurably more lives than the stepped-up regime of traffic ticketing.

Studies show that, in some contexts, increasing the number of traffic tickets will reduce traffic accidents and accident-related injuries.[53] But, as Priya Sarathy Jones, national policy director of the Fines and Fees Justice Center, reports, "there's little evidence that the *amou*nt of a traffic fine—and definitely not the amount of a traffic *fee*—has any impact on traffic safety. There's a little bit of research that we've looked at that could indicate that there is potentially a use for a *small* fine, but there's definitely no evidence that a $1,000 fine is more effective than, say, a $10 fine in deterring dangerous behavior." Nevertheless, any cost accounting of police enforcement, she insists, should include "all of the dangerous things that can happen during an armed, human traffic stop."[54]

Safe-street advocates look to the physical redesign of roads, especially through traffic-calming features like daylighting or traffic circles, as the preferred solution for enforcement. After the "right of way" was won for cars in the early twentieth century, the growth of auto-centric infrastructure resulted in a gross imbalance between drivers and pedestrians, and an invitation to drive recklessly. Designing and implementing self-enforcing streets would help rectify that disparity and might eventually replace the current alternative of automated enforcement through red light cameras, which city managers greatly favor as a cheap and highly efficient way of generating revenue.[55] The doctrine of Vision Zero, a model pioneered in Sweden and adopted by many U.S. cities, holds that injuries, crashes, and deaths are not "accidents" but the result of failed street design. Vision Zero aims at eliminating them entirely through a combination of engineering, education, and enforcement.

Civil rights advocates have criticized Vision Zero as lacking in equity—a fourth kind of e-word—and especially in its practical over-reliance on enforcement, which is supposed to be a last resort, and targeted only at visibly dangerous driving. Evidence shows that, even under Vision Zero, the policing of reckless driving still lags behind ticketing for minor infractions in low-income neighborhoods. For example, one study found that, in thirty-two New York City precincts, officers issued more tickets for tinted windows than for speeding and failure to yield combined; in the predominantly African American neighborhood of Brownsville, over a four month period, 1,257 summonses were issued for tinted windows and only 85 for failure to yield.[56] Nor has the policy resulted in a reduction of pedestrian and cyclist fatalities.[57] Technocratic strategies like Vision Zero have a hard time stamping out racist and lucrative policing habits that annually generate as many as thirty million cases for relatively minor infractions and misdemeanors punishable by fines and fees.[58]

The mountain of debt generated by these cases is illustrative of what social theorists call the *carceral state*. Mass imprisonment is obviously the central element of a society characterized by a strong penchant for punishment. Even in the current era of drawdown, the U.S. is still a "nation of criminals," holding by far the largest known incarcerated population in the world, with more than 2.3 million people in prison or jail.[59] But the carceral techniques of discipline and correction extend far beyond the vast archipelago of American jails and prisons. As Michel Foucault and others have argued, many of these are techniques of social control, saturating the mentality of institutional life, while others are fiscal feedlots for government operations that include the criminal justice system among others. In our view, debt generated by the likes of traffic fines and fees fulfills both functions, and the capacity of the state to act, at one and the same time, as enforcer, judge, punisher, debt collector, and creditor ensures that both are administered in sufficient quantities.

On the one hand, the issuance of LFOs, backed by the threat of license suspension and incarceration, draws large segments of the population into the orbit of close social regulation and surveillance, curtailing their freedoms and mobility. Additional penalties for nonpayment serve as reminders of the punishment that awaits delinquents. On the other hand, the ascendancy of the low-tax mentality has forced local and state governments to debt-finance their enterprises, and so they seek to fulfill their responsibilities to creditors by harvesting funds from constituents in lieu of higher taxes.[60] In addition to the lucrative collections and bail industries, the outsourcing of components of the criminal justice system to private companies generates additional opportunities to extract revenue, especially from the captive prison retail market; phone calls, commissaries, and money transfers are large debt generators that extend across social networks. "When we go to prison, we become another bill [for our families]," as one formerly incarcerated man put it. "Just another bill," his friend agreed, repeating the phrase for emphasis.

With the prison population on the decline since 2009, the political class may be losing its appetite for mass incarceration. But even as jails and prisons are shuttered, the carceral state is alive and well in undertakings, including the imposition of legal debt in cases that do not involve actual convictions. Sociologist Issa Kohler-Hausmann points out that misdemeanors for petty violations like traffic offenses account for by far the most cases processed by the criminal legal system. Defendants sentenced for such violations end up in jail, not prison, but even these conviction rates are falling. In what she calls "misdemeanorland," about half of the cases are dismissed, but offenders are humiliated and degraded, and taught obedience to dispassionate rules, while their time and energy is consumed through the interminable procedures of the courts.[61] Each year, several million people pass through this dragnet of discipline. Countless others must dig themselves out of the LFO debt trap by ensnaring themselves in predatory civil debt.

At this point, the high human cost of fines and fees is well-documented, and it has prompted abolitionists to action.[62] In various states, advocates have won piecemeal reforms of legislation. After San Francisco eliminated criminal administrative fees and discharged outstanding debt in June 2018, Debt Free Justice California successfully lobbied Alameda, Contra Costa, and Los Angeles counties to follow suit. California is also the first state to end money bail. California passed Assembly Bill 1869 in September 2020 to eliminate twenty-three criminal administrative fees across the state, and to discharge more than $16 billion in outstanding fee debt.[63]

Colorado, Mississippi, Washington, Massachusetts, and Michigan have passed bills mandating or guiding judges to assess ability to pay during hearings. In 2020, Hawaii, Maryland, Oregon, Virginia, and West Virginia joined New York in passing reforms of license suspensions and, in 2021, Michigan, Illinois, Utah, and Arkansas passed similar measures. Amnesty periods are more frequently offered for debtors who cannot pay. Traffic stops are on the decline, arguably in response to critical public scrutiny. Indeed, several of our older interviewees reported that they had seen the frequency of such stops diminish over the years. Significantly, however, statistical evidence shows a smaller decline in stops, searches, and arrests of women than in the case of men.[64]

As for traffic fines and fees, the pandemic lockdown saw a large drop in ticketing, though these numbers have been on the decline for some time, partly due to cuts in police staffing. Not surprisingly, however, that downturn has been offset by a rise in the average fine, augmented by hikes in surcharges and supplementary fees as local and state government officials look to refill their depleted coffers. Defiant in the face of Supreme Court judgements that have upheld the Excessive Fines Clause, the Equal Protection Clause, and the nineteenth-century bans on debt peonage and debtors' prisons, our expectation is that sub-federal authorities will continue to find ways of protecting the carceral goose that lays so many golden eggs.

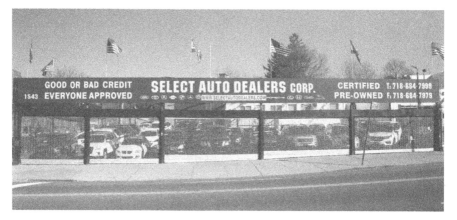

Debt trap lying in wait.

Chapter Four

Why Do So Many Owe So Much?

Usury lives in the pores of production...just as the gods of Epicurus lived in the space between the worlds.

—*Karl Marx, Capital (Vol. III)*

The business media issues periodic warnings about the looming threat of an "auto debt bubble" by drawing analogies with the subprime housing crash of 2008.[1] Most of these stories are aimed at the overheated mindset of readers who are finance junkies, but the forecasts still look ominous. Unlike with student loans and housing debt payments, there was no provision for auto debt forbearance under the 2020 CARES Act during the pandemic, nor did any of the federal moratoriums (on evictions, for example) extend to car repossession. Households in deep economic hardship had some respite from paying rent or education loans and so they were able to keep their cars on the road. After the moratoriums in many states ran out in the fall of 2020, the volume of subprime borrowers with car loans more than sixty days overdue saw straight monthly gains.[2]

When the federal moratoriums and boosted unemployment benefits ended in the summer of 2021, household budgets got squeezed even harder, and the K-shaped recovery began to take its toll on the lower socioeconomic half of the population. Delinquencies on auto loans of all classes began to rise and collections fell. Repo men, equipped with the latest license plate–recognition cameras, saw a bonanza in the making.[3] Meanwhile, auto makers faced with an unforeseen microchip shortage were unable to meet the post-pandemic appetite for new cars. Sticker prices jumped as the demand for all kinds of vehicles soared, heralding a new round of high-risk borrowing for owners and turbo-boosted profits for lenders who can now flip repossessed cars at higher prices than their book value.[4]

The long-term figures are just as disturbing. As one man we interviewed put it, "Everyone's in debt. It's the American way." Nationally, the amount owed on car loans increased by a whopping 85 percent in the decade after 2009, second only to student loans, which rose 107 percent. The fastest growth (127 percent) was among subprime borrowers, the population most likely to default. By June 2022, the aggregates stood at $1.47 trillion for auto debt, and $1.75 trillion for student debt, while the average debts were $40,000 for new cars (and $28,000 for used cars), and $30,000 for student loans. (Medical debt, now owed by 50 percent of Americans, may total as much as $1 trillion.)[5] But the numbers of those burdened by such high debt loads show a marked, racial disparity. Also, due to auto-dependency in the U.S., there are more than twice as many people with auto loans or leases as there are student loan borrowers. As for housing loans, which account for the lion's share of household debt, there are only 80.75 million mortgage holders, while there are more than 112 million car loan accounts.[6]

While auto debt and student debt are on roughly the same upward curve, only the latter has figured in the public mind as a problem that merits drastic government action in the form of mass debt cancellation. Activists are largely responsible for the high profile of the student debt crisis, but their capacity to sway opinion rests on a well-established perception that higher education is a public good, if not a right, and that it is immoral to pile such a heavy load on those learning much-needed knowledge and skills.[7] Of course, transportation is also a public good, but its public component has never been adequately funded. The vast proportion of the federal transportation budget, as much as four-fifths, still goes to subsidizing private travel on roads and highways. As a result of the Biden administration's

Infrastructure Bill, the historic 80 to 20 percent split between private and public transit was further skewed to 82 and 18 percent. In most parts of the US, the dearth of mass transit means that a personal car is a sheer necessity. And, unlike housing and education loans, which can credibly be seen as investments with foreseeable returns, auto loans are "bad debt," amassed on an asset that depreciates in value the moment it is purchased. Yet the pleasure and status associated with cars keeps them classed as a luxury in the popular imagination, and there is little moral outrage about how and why driving a car has become such a tightly sprung debt trap, unevenly afflicting lower-income and minority drivers.

Nor has the continuum between auto ownership and incarceration—the topic of this book—received much attention, let alone afforded a foothold in mainstream consciousness. The vast carbon footprint of U.S. auto-dependence has become a prime target for climate justice warriors, and rightly so. Yet the ease with which gas-guzzling vehicles can be financed these days is partly to blame. If you have poor credit and scant income, it is still more straightforward to buy a fuel-inefficient SUV or sedan than to find a rental apartment. In this chapter, we focus on the conditions of that purchase and its often dire consequences for those who have no other option but to take on a serious debt load just to be mobile.

Since more than 87 percent of new cars (and 34.5 percent of used vehicles) are bought with borrowed money, ownership is hardly a recipe for financial freedom.[8] The psychological leeway provided by "creative financing," and the skullduggery deployed to arrange it, means that buyers routinely drive off the lot in cars with price and maintenance costs far beyond their means. No other asset loses value so rapidly, or is so commonly financed by such loosely regulated lenders, prone to predatory practices. As a result, many owners never succeed in paying off their debt. They end up being "upside down" on their loans, meaning that they owe more for the car than it is worth, and so they fold the balance into another loan for a new vehicle. Lenders show little leniency if they fall behind on payments. Indeed, many expect borrowers to default, and so repossession is invariably the next step, allowing dealers to sell the car to the next sap. Even if the surrender of the vehicle is voluntary, drivers take a big hit on their credit scores, making that next car loan more expensive and their debt hole even deeper. Yet there is no alternative. The prospect of living and trying to find work in most parts of the US. without a car is a much harsher economic penalty.

Nor is that the only punishment in the offing. A jail sentence is also a potential outcome, depending on the tenacity of a debt collector, or the indifference of a judge. The traffic fines we reviewed in the previous chapter are not the only kind of car-related debt that can lead to incarceration. In the case of auto debt, it is not an ill-fated interaction with a police officer but a soured relationship with a lender that may result in jail time. One sets a speed trap, the other a debt trap, but both lie in wait for those who fall for the head-turner in the manufacturer's impossibly seductive ad or who fancy the retro look of an older model in the used-car dealer's lot. It is an especially bitter irony that these promises of stylish or reliable independence on the road do double duty as contracts that deprive so many of their financial and physical liberty. To be sure, this is not the result of technological engineering; it is in large part the outcome of social and political decision-making that allows the financing arm of the car industry to treat consumers as chumps, or at best as captive, and thus vulnerable, consumers of an indispensable product.

Truth in Lending?

There are many nutty things that people do with their cars, but abandoning expensive ones is usually not among them. Yet, in Dubai, the spectacle of deserted supercars is a common sight in streets, parking garages, and airport lots. Several thousand Ferraris, Bugattis, Porsches, Koenigseggs, Bentleys, Lamborghinis, Audis, and BMWs are discarded and left to gather sandy dust every year. Their owners borrowed heavily to live large and are now in over their heads. Under UAE law, failure to pay debts is a criminal offense, and car owners cannot transfer their titles to someone else unless they have first paid off their loans.[9] With no bankruptcy option available either, they are faced with doing time in one of the nation's notoriously grim jails. The only alternative is to walk away from their luxury rides and flee the country.

The UAE is not the only country in the Middle East where it is perilous to default on a debt. Despite being a signatory to the Arab Human Rights Charter, which prohibits the criminalization of debtors, Saudi Arabia leans heavily on Sharia law to do so.[10] In Jordan, roughly 12 percent of the prison population were locked up for debt delinquency in 2019.[11] But the corollary of this harsh regimen is that Islamic religious practice has a strong anti-usury component; it is forbidden to collect or benefit from interest (*riba*) on a loan. There are several Sharia-compliant ways of financing assets (whereby creditors and borrowers share risks and profits), but the bar on usurious loans acts as a general check on predatory conduct. Debtors can be imprisoned but it is less likely that their debts are extortionate or that they have been fleeced by creditors who know they cannot pay.

In the U.S., where usury has lost its status as a civil sin and become almost respectable, the intersection between law and the finance industry is quite a different matter. Technically speaking, no one can be imprisoned for failing to pay civil debts, though, as we will see, many end up behind bars because their creditors are allowed to exploit loopholes in the legal process. There are just as many loopholes in the patchwork of state usury laws that have evolved ever since the original thirteen colonies placed interest caps (between 5 and 8 percent) on lending. Today, general usury limits range from 7 percent in Michigan to 45 percent in Colorado and Oklahoma, while there are no general usury rates in Nevada and New Hampshire.[12] Many states have special carve-outs for auto loans, allowing APRs to go much higher, and, in some, they are exempt from the usury caps. Notwithstanding these statutory limits, desperate consumers often privately agree to higher rates. In doing so, they waive, unwittingly or not, the protections afforded by law. Many others are bamboozled by the many deceptive ways by which the cost of credit is calculated, including the packing of hidden fees into the total loan amount and not the finance charge. The "real" APRs turn out to be more typical of predatory payday lending, ranging from 75 to 300 percent and higher.[13]

These private agreements, exemptions, and forms of concealed usury are more likely to occur in the business of purchasing a car. Unlike student and mortgage loans, which involve some degree of involvement on the part of government agencies as direct lenders or insurers, auto financing is a wholly private and unsecured market. The federal government collects very little data on this market, and there are no federal rate limits. The reluctance of many states to set or properly regulate limits adds to the climate of abusive rate-setting. In the absence of adequate oversight, borrowers and lenders are more at liberty to ignore the statutory limits in the interest of making a deal. But even without these private workarounds, the complicated structure of an auto loan transaction makes it easy to exceed state usury caps.[14]

Take New York, which, relative to other states, has an upright reputation for keeping loan sharks in line. It prohibits payday loans, the most exploitative form of poverty lending, and its 16 percent interest cap (up from 6 percent in 1717) is somewhere in the middle of the national spectrum. Charging more than 25 percent for consumer loans in New York is considered a felony, yet it is not uncommon for car buyers with lower credit scores to be charged such excessively high rates when they sign a retail installment sales contract (RIC) with a dealer, thereby committing themselves to a fixed number of payments over time—plus a "finance charge"—for the vehicle. These exorbitant rates are legal because, technically, an RIC is not a loan.

Typically, the dealer will sell the RIC to a bank or financial institution, which is then entitled to collect principal and interest payments as an "indirect lender." These creditors could not legally lend directly to customers at rates that exceed the usury cap, but they can do so when they buy auto RICs. The dealer takes a cut of the financial profit—a markup on the buy rate—but the right to collect the lion's share of the returns belongs to the external lender. Under 1980 amendments to the Motor Vehicle Retail Installment Sales Act, New York authorized dealers to set higher RIC rates than the previous limits of 7 percent for new cars and 13 percent for used cars, while the caps on refinancing charges and late payment fees were lifted. The outcome was a jump in the number of contracts signed with interest rates above the 16 percent civil usury cap, and a steady increase in those signed at 24.99 percent, just shy of the criminal usury rate, ensuring that many borrowers at these rates are actually paying more interest than the cost of the car. In 2018, Santander, one of the biggest subprime lenders, offered Wall Street investors a bundle of loans for securitization. Fifty-seven percent were over the civil cap, and some were in violation of the criminal cap rate.[15]

Dealers and lenders operate like a tag team, trading off liability to evade closer regulation. Conveniently, the National Automobile Dealers Association lobbied hard to get dealerships carved out of the federal Consumer Financial Protection Bureau (CFPB), set up after the 2008 crash, on the premise that the cratering auto industry was too weak to withstand tougher oversight. The result was a gift to lenders, who call the shots in most auto transactions, and for whom the dealer is a willing front man. Dealers are still required to be compliant with a myriad of federal laws, including the Truth in Lending Act, Federal Consumer Leasing Act, Equal Credit Opportunity Act, and the Fair Credit Reporting Act, but the seasoned rituals of hustling and haggling that await anyone who walks onto a car dealer's lot are crafted to obscure the fact that the lender is driving the deal. So, too, because the existing regulation of dealers is split between state agencies, the Federal Trade Commission, and the Federal Reserve, responsibility for grossly usurious deals is more difficult to detect and easier to evade.

The industry protocols that bind dealers and lenders in a monopoly have survived intact for many decades and are only now being challenged by fintech companies that offer customers online loan options. Virtual financing may well "disrupt" this intimate relationship by offering buyers more choices, but that does not guarantee better deals. It is just as likely to provide a more effective method for the auto industry to evade state usury caps. This slippery practice originated with the landmark 1978 Supreme Court decision *Marquette National Bank of Minneapolis v. First of Omaha Service Corp.* that barred states from applying anti-usury laws to nationally chartered banks based in another state with looser regulations. The result was a massive windfall for the finance industry and the credit card business in particular, allowing banks that subsequently relocated to South Dakota and Delaware to issue credit products to anyone in the U.S. at unrestricted interest rates. Today, many states allow auto lenders to set interest rates based on the usury cap of where the creditor is headquartered.

Marquette's relaxation of usury oversight set off a competitive wave of financial deregulation that lasted for almost three decades. Within two years, the federal Depository Institutions Deregulation and Monetary Control Act had eliminated interest-rate caps on deposits, and then in 1982 the Alternative Mortgage Transaction Parity Act lifted restrictions on the use of variable interest rates and balloon payments on mortgage loans.[16] The latter fueled the rise of the subprime mortgage loan that brought the financial industry to its knees in 2008. After the crash, subprime lending entered the auto loan industry with a vengeance. As with the pre-2008 housing loans, the penetration of subprime (for credit scores of 600 or lower) was a direct response to income stagnation among working- and middle-class households, further squeezed by the austerity ushered in by the Great Recession.

But the growth of subprime lending was also accelerated by the rapid emergence of a market in auto asset-backed securities (ABS), not unlike the mortgage-backed securities and collateralized debt obligations that had brought on the crash. Keen investor demand for these risky but high-yield bonds motivated lenders to actively seek out new borrowers so that their debts could be bundled into securities. Not surprisingly, this led to looser credit and underwriting standards as creditors glossed over consumers' ability to pay in the rush to sign up loan contracts. In 2019, for example, Moody's found that Santander verified the income of less than 3 percent of the borrowers whose loans it sold to investors in the form of bonds.[17]

Car Rich, Cash Poor

Santander and the other large subprime lenders like Ally Financial, Wells Fargo, Capital One, Fifth Third Bank, Toyota Financial Services, and Credit Acceptance Corporation (the last considered the most rapacious of all) operate in a marketplace that is a final resort for borrowers with low credit ratings and unstable sources of income. Aside from the risk of lawsuits— and these companies are regularly sued—their business involves surprisingly few risks and hefty profits. If borrowers cannot repay, repossessing the car is quick and easy since sticker prices are often inflated for subprime borrowers; the actual cost of servicing a loan can be at least twice as much as the real value of the car. Borrowers must pay the fees for repossession, storage, and preparation for reselling the vehicle, while the proceeds from resale go toward their already inflated deficiency balance. Credit Acceptance, the prince of thieves, reportedly repossesses 35 percent of the cars it finances, and although it operates on the assumption that it will collect only about 70 percent of the money it lends, including from repossession, deficiency collection, and wage and income tax garnishment, it still reaps 40 percent of its return.[18] A research report on the company's business model concluded that "Credit Acceptance is a new kind of hybrid: a debt collector that originates its own loans—a combination that has proved extraordinarily profitable for investors as the business of lending to troubled borrowers has surged since the financial crisis."[19]

Credit Acceptance also helped to pioneer the installation of starter kill switches and GPS locators so that the company could incapacitate or track vehicles remotely in the event of a missed payment. With such systems, any grace period is easily eliminated, and drivers can be suddenly stranded by the side of the road, waiting for electronic payments to clear. As one of our interviewees commented, "it'll cut off anywhere" no matter how inconvenient. Advertising its services with corny slogans like "Everyone Deserves a Second Chance," the ruthless methods Credit Acceptance deploys to extract every last dime from customers have attracted fierce legal scrutiny in dozens of states and inspired a mountain of consumer complaints to the CFPB.[20] Each time it faces an investigation (in as many as forty-three states and counting) or lawsuit, these unscrupulous practices are fully exposed. But the often-hefty settlements are regarded as the cost of doing business. A 2021 Massachusetts suit argued that Credit Acceptance levied hidden charges that added from 37 to 68 percent to loans for customers with low credit scores, resulting in an actual interest rate higher than the Massachusetts usury ceiling of 21 percent.[21] The borrowers were also required to buy expensive vehicle service contracts that inflated their loans, and were harassed by eight phone calls a day from the company's collectors, far above the state's legal limit of two.[22] More damaging to its stock price, Credit Acceptance and its executives were sued for violating federal securities laws by failing to disclose to investors that they were topping off its pools of packaged and securitized loans with higher-risk loans.[23] Shares in the company took a big hit (an 18-percent fall in two days) after it agreed to the Massachusetts court settlement. A few months earlier when New York's attorney general showed interest in a similar suit, Steve Eisman, the Wall Street portfolio manager who famously bet against subprime housing loans before the 2008 crash, declared that Credit Acceptance was now his biggest short.[24]

Anticipating more lawsuits and crackdowns, Wall Street might well desert one or more of the high-flying subprime lenders, but the problem of predatory auto-financing extends well beyond a few bad apples. A long-established system that protects the regional networks of auto dealerships ensures that the lengthy showroom hustle universally despised by buyers will continue. As readers will see when we describe Jumaane's loan later in the book, the deception often begins with bait-and-switch advertising, when a car promoted at a come-on price turns out to be more expensive on the lot or unavailable. Once customers are on-site, the trickery intensifies, especially if it is a "sign and drive" business, enticing them with the prospect of driving off the lot (a "spot delivery") without actually having to write a check.

The dealer's standard opening line, "How much do you want to pay for a car?" is crafted to initiate a lengthy process of negotiations riddled with emotional triggers to hook consumers into an impulse buy. A common dictum among salespeople is that "the buyer is a liar."[25] Customers profess to know what they want, but invariably walk out with something that is quite different, loaded with features and accessories they have never even heard of but that seem to fit with the sense of self they will project through the car. If they drive off the lot that day, they are often ensnared in a scam known as a yo-yo—forced to return the car and negotiate a higher loan when the dealer reports that the initially proposed financing deal is no longer available.

Buyers with tarnished credit scores (almost guaranteed for anyone with a recent criminal record) are especially at risk of ending up, after several hours of wrangling, with signed paperwork that is packed with made-up fees and add-ons. These supplements are presented as if they are built into the loan package; extended warranties, gap insurance, window etching, roadside assistance, service contracts, rustproofing, and protection packages for everything including keys, tires, wheels, paint and fabric, etc. With the add-ons, which is where dealerships make most of their profits, the sum payment may be twice as much as the car costs the dealer, and, if they walk out with a long-term loan, buyers are likely to be "upside down" before it matures.[26] The last decade has seen the full-throttle promotion of such long-term loans, peddled by an industry bent on persuading consumers to purchase high-status cars with "luxury" accessories that they can't afford. In the second quarter of 2020, Experian reported that the average term of a new car loan exceeded 72 months for the first time[27] and, by the first quarter of 2021, more than 32 percent of car shoppers were signing loans for between 73 and 84 months, with the average new car loan term for those with subprime credit scores at 73.36 months.[28] These long-term loans all but guarantee a steady increase in the number of borrowers who owe more to lenders than their car is worth. As a result, owners are holding on to their cars for longer, but when they reach the point of being upside down, they roll over their old debt into a new car loan, adding to their payment burden. In 2020, a whopping 44 percent of all traded-in vehicles were carrying negative equity.[29]

Relative to income, cars have gotten considerably more expensive over the last four decades. According to the Consumer Price Index of the U.S. Bureau of Labor Statistics, prices for new cars were 84.6 percent higher in 2021 than they were in 1975, when the average US working wage began to stagnate.[30] For the vast majority, then, the seemingly insatiable (ideological) appetite for a big American vehicle can only be met by financing or leasing. By 2020, 87 percent of new cars were being financed, and 18 percent of those were purchased with subprime loans, at rates five times higher than prime.[31] At that time, the average subprime loan, which is frequently offered at a (more risky) variable and not a fixed rate, was $31,190, while the average prime loan was $37,431.[32] Not surprisingly, the percentage of these subprime loans that lead to default, or negative equity, is much higher than with prime, and is disproportionately higher among minority owners, many of whom are targeted precisely because they are more likely to default (an example of what Keeanga-Yamahtta Taylor, referring to housing loans, calls "predatory inclusion").[33]

Notwithstanding the explosive growth of subprime auto lending since 2010, car manufacturers have long recognized the superior profitability of financing. In fact, cars were the prototypes for debt-driven extraction long before the "age of financialization." In the 1920s, General Motors delivered the quintessential business school lesson when it overhauled Ford's hefty sales lead by offering auto financing as part of an arrangement that shared the risk of car loans between dealer and manufacturer. Though its initial goal was simply to move product more swiftly, the firm soon found the financing to be a more lucrative business than the selling of cars themselves. These profits were magnified by "planned obsolescence," GM's other innovation in capitalist salesmanship. Persuaded that they needed a new upgraded model periodically to maintain their status, consumers were assured that the General Motors Acceptance Corporation (GMAC) would provide the loans they needed to keep up. The formula was so successful that GMAC diversified over time, moving into vehicle insurance, mortgages, direct banking, financial trading, and private equity. Ford and Chrysler followed suit, along with the other large captive lenders in the auto industry, to grab their share of the expanding credit market.

But cars are not the only vehicle-related assets for which financing is on offer. Accounting for 20 percent of global total automotive revenues, the "aftermarket," composed of service and retail parts, is invariably the most profitable sector of the carmaker's industry.[34] So, in addition to purchase and leasing loans, there is a busy market in credit for auto repair loans; auto parts loans; wheel, tire, and rim loans; and even battery loans. If your transmission breaks down, someone will offer you a loan for a new one too. All these niche markets are booming. Rent-A-Tire/Rent-A-Wheel is one of the fastest-growing businesses in the entire rent-to-own sector. For those living paycheck to paycheck, renting a new set of tires is the only way to stay on the road, but they may end up paying three times as much for them, and one missed payment will almost certainly result in repossession of the tires.

Car title loans are arguably the most predatory of all, marketed as emergency short-term funding for those who own their cars clear and free. Annually, as many as two million owners in desperate need of cash use their cars as collateral and hand over the title and duplicate set of keys in return for a loan with sky-high interest rates of 300 percent APR on average. The loan typically needs to be repaid in a single balloon payment after a month. For those unable to make the payment, loans can be renewed for a stiff fee, laying the groundwork, eventually, for repossession. According to the CFPB, 80 percent of borrowers renew their loans on the day they are due, and one in five end up having their vehicle seized by the lender.[35]

In response to criticism about a racket designed to defraud those with few options, lobbyists for the finance industry argue that subprime and aftermarket lenders provide a lifeline for low-income consumers with no ready access to public transit and no prospect of employment without their own wheels.[36] This is largely true. But lenders are hardly motivated by a gallant desire to help the downtrodden—they are in business because the demographic in question is the easiest to exploit, with high profit margins guaranteed. As with other debt classes, poorer households end up paying much more for cars, auto loans, and vehicle insurance than they should, and the evidence of racial discrimination in lending is quite clear.[37]

African American borrowers are charged more on all of these loan products at dealerships. A 2015 National Consumer Law Center study showed large markups on their loans in every state and region; 200 percent increases were common, but some clocked in at more than 500 percent. In one case, a Primus (Ford) dealership in Wisconsin was found to have charged a 667 percent markup for Black borrowers.[38] The financing arms of Toyota, Honda, and GM are among those forced to pay settlements for discriminating against African American and Latinx customers in this way. In 2017, a study in auto insurance redlining by ProPublica and Consumer

Reports found that some insurers were charging premiums that were on average 30 percent higher in zip codes where most residents are minorities than in whiter neighborhoods with similar accident costs.[39]

Extortionate sales conduct is endemic to the dealership and auto financing system, but fraud is even more prevalent in used car sales. The worst shakedowns occur in "Buy Here, Pay Here" (BHPH) lots that sell cheap, high-mileage vehicles at prices above the Blue Book value to strapped consumers with little or no credit rating. These largely unregulated outlets are generally located in neighborhoods with households under extreme financial stress, and they sit on the same "Loan Alley" strip as payday lenders, pawnshops, and check-cashing facilities. Traditionally, BHPHs were "mom and pop" dealerships, but this sector is no longer unconnected to the mainstream of the finance industry. Like payday lenders and check-cashing outlets, many are now consolidated and backed by Wall Street investors or bondholders, and especially the larger subprime chains like America's Car Mart, CarMax, ByRider, and DriveTime, which also offer BHPH terms.

According to the National Alliance of Buy Here Pay Here Dealers, BHPH shops reaped an average profit of 38 percent in 2020, double the profit margin of conventional retail car chains.[40] Not surprisingly, these lavish returns have attracted private equity and hedge fund investors. The key to the profits is that financing is done in-house, executed by salespeople who take full advantage of the fact that the deep subprime buyers who walk on to the lot are so unbackable they cannot get a loan anywhere else and are usually in urgent need of a vehicle. While they know they will be gouged, consumers have good reasons to fear being carless. Several of our interviewees broke down the terms for us and commented that such practices were "just not right." Jeff, a white, recently released, Indiana resident, acknowledged that the car loan he took on was "predatory" but explained that "had to do it in order to get to work and my probation meetings and things like that."

Loan-to-Jail Pipeline

Formerly incarcerated buyers are more likely to fall into the category of highly vulnerable consumers. If they serve a long sentence, they either have no recent credit history, or their credit defaults and delinquencies have piled up because of their inability to repay loans while behind bars. On release, they are often saddled with accumulated carceral debt, and the grueling search for employment is generally dependent on access to a car. So, too, scheduled meetings with a parole or probation officer are often in locations far from reliable public transit. Reacquiring a license and securing a vehicle are top priorities on reentry. The social pressure to show to the world that you are bouncing back often translates into a high-interest loan agreement on an expensive model, like the one that Jeff signed. But all too often, the condition of being "car rich and cash poor" sets the owner up for more interactions with the criminal justice system when debt repayment is only possible through illegal economic activity.

While auto dealers and lenders commit fraud on a routine basis, they are much less likely to end up behind bars than those to whom they peddle cars through their con games and high-pressure sales tactics. Any lawyer will tell you that it is illegal in the US to be arrested or jailed for failing to pay consumer debts, but there are dozens of states in which civil debtors do find themselves behind bars or threatened with jail time. The driving force in these situations are debt collectors, either working directly for the lender or as third-party enforcers.[41] Although they are regulated by federal and state consumer collection laws, and by the Fair Debt Collection Practice Act, which prohibits collectors from using the threat of criminal prosecution for failing to pay a debt, creditors and their enforcers still find it remarkably easy to manipulate the justice system to incarcerate delinquent borrowers.

That opportunity arises when judges, at the request of collection agencies, issue arrest warrants for failure to appear in court on unpaid civil debt judgments. Debtors face arrest and jail time not for the delinquency itself, but for contempt of court. From their perspective, however, the distinction doesn't make a whole lot of difference. There are forty-four states that allow this to happen, even when it is obvious that debtors cannot pay, or when their debts are still being disputed. The practice, which also includes incarceration for unpaid child support or divorce proceedings, is so common that the lead author of a 2018 ACLU report on the criminalization of private debt declared that the "courts have been completely co-opted by the debt-collection industry."[42]

With a willing prosecutor or judge, the process is relatively straightforward. In civil court, a creditor obtains a money judgment against a debtor who cannot pay off an auto loan or car title loan (a small secured loan that uses your car as collateral). Debtors are represented by lawyers in just 2 percent of such cases according to the Federal Trade Commission, so it is not surprising that debt collectors win 95 percent of those cases. The court can issue a wage garnishment order or otherwise authorize the seizure of assets, including from bank account funds. If collectors still cannot extract enough to cover the loan balance, they can ask the court to schedule a post-judgement debtor's examination, ostensibly to inquire about the borrower's finances. Sometimes, multiple exam orders are requested in order to apply pressure and in anticipation of a no-show sooner or later. If or when debtors fail to respond to an order to appear, they are found to be in civil contempt, and in as many as forty-four states that allow judges to do so, an arrest warrant can follow. Those who end up in jail are required to post a bond that typically corresponds to the amount of the debt. Though technically arrested for contempt, in effect they are behind bars for a debt they cannot pay; and they are on the hook for the balance plus interest, and invariably additional court fines, surcharges, and collection fees.

In many states, an increasingly prevalent tactic deployed by payday and car title lenders is to sue delinquent borrowers under a "bad check" or "theft by check" law. Typically, these kinds of creditors require borrowers to provide a postdated check or access to their bank account in order to secure a loan. When the account cannot cover the amount of the check, they are sued for fraud or theft. The violation may then be treated as a misdemeanor, carrying a potential jail sentence, but it can also be considered a felony if the sum is large enough.

In a 2020 study of Utah courts, the Consumer Federation of America found that high-cost lenders who used these and other tactics were dominating small-claims court dockets, and were the most aggressive plaintiffs, suing over smaller amounts and litigating for much longer than other plaintiffs. The median debt in dispute was as low as $994, and three out of ten high-cost lender lawsuits resulted in a bench warrant for the arrest of the borrower for contempt of court. The report concluded that "small-claims courts—originally designed to improve access to justice for average Americans—are now primarily used by usurious lenders to aggressively collect triple-digit interest rates from poor, insolvent borrowers."[43] Studies in other states showed a similar increase in the volume of criminal charges being filed for relatively small loan amounts, and a pattern of disproportionately targeting debtors of color.[44]

For most debtors who find themselves funneled into this debt-to-jail pipeline, their only real misdeed is their poverty. They are legally hounded and punished *because, and in spite of,* their hardship, and are deprived of their liberty for small sums of money that can be spun into larger, and more profitable, liabilities through the court process. While only a minority of these judgments result in defendants serving jail time, the threat of incarceration is an extremely effective way of forcing debtors to seek out funds to make their payments, indirectly encouraging actual criminal activity. In addition to escaping effective regulation themselves, debt collectors and predatory lenders can leverage powers far beyond their own command by using the courts as an aggressive enforcement weapon in this way. These tactics are just as immoral (and often illegal) as the scams they pull to get borrowers to sign costly loans padded with add-ons. The consumers they choose to target have the least resources and yet they are burned the most.

By contrast, auto buyers who can afford to pay up front or secure cheap loans have the smoothest ride.

Indebtedness should not ever lead to detention, and the loopholes and back doors that creditors find at their disposal should be firmly closed off. But even in the absence of an arrest threat, car debt is itself a powerful form of social discipline and control. While auto loans are now the price of our access to physical mobility, the steep cost of their debt service sets limits on other forms of mobility, constraining their financial choices and enforcing social norms about unswerving obedience to defrauding creditors. For most of us, our cars, no matter how much we cherish them, hold us in social and economic custody. As more and more vehicles are financed and with higher loans and interest rates, creditors exert a carceral pull over our budgets and our ability to earn a sustainable livelihood. Perhaps the most telling evidence of this servitude is that, in times of financial stress, households will prioritize their monthly car payments over all others, including basic necessities. Surely this is the mark of our perverse civilization when food, medical care, and housing have to take a back seat to our need to keep wheels on the road.

Yet this is the natural outcome of a creditocracy, where indebtedness becomes the precondition not just for material improvements in the quality of life, but for the basic requirements of life: where one in three Americans with a credit record are pursued by debt collectors;[45] where fear of a damaged credit score governs our conduct; and where the ideal citizens are "revolvers," who fail to make monthly payments and resort to rolling over their debts, with penalties, ensuring they are kept on the hook as revenue generators indefinitely.[46] Even more than housing, which is still by far the single largest component of household debt, the acquisition and use of cars engenders multiple kinds of debt service; for purchase, repairs, licensing, maintenance, insurance, traffic violations, court fines and fees, and medical costs in the event of accidents. The result is a rolling feast of revenue for creditors in each of these sectors, with the full force of the courts to back up the extraction of profit.

By contrast, for many if not most owners, the compounding costs and risks to legal exposure of owning a private vehicle would surely outweigh its economic benefits if it were not such a necessary asset. First and foremost, there is the depreciating value of the car. In a few cases, the art of custom modifying ("modding") a car can raise its value, but it's just as likely to hurt resale since it can alter the design integrity of the vehicle. Second, there is the draining experience of paying back more than the car's original worth or of prolonging the losses through rolling over the balance into a new loan on another car. Then there is a significant risk of a sheer loss, in the form of a crash or a repossession. And, at the end of it all, the equally ruinous prospect of a jail sentence. All things considered, when compared to the choices available in a capitalist economy, few other investments in physical assets (with the exception, perhaps, of yachts) are such a losing proposition. Yet it is probably the only one we cannot afford to reject.

Public and Private

Because the subprime auto lenders are among the least-regulated members of the creditor class, debtor advocacy groups are focused on reforms that reduce the harms they impose on low-income households: stronger regulation of dealers and lenders; lowering usury caps; and stricter observance of the bar on debtors' prisons. The same organizations are sometimes active in the fines and fees movement, bent on lessening the impact of traffic debt and LFOs incurred within the criminal justice system. But their advocacy work tends to respect the partitioning of these two debt classes—auto loans and traffic fines—into civil and criminal realms. This segregation of legal jurisdictions reflects a constitutive difference between the rights and responsibilities of private lenders in the business of auto financing and state creditors in the enforcement of traffic codes. Yet from the perspective of car owners, this distinction is less relevant, especially since both kinds of debt are common by-products of auto-dependence and both can lead to legal jeopardy in the courts and the carceral system. As for how these obligations are handled, our interviews showed that the two are tightly interwoven in the everyday financial lives of consumers; the source of the debt is less important than the exigency of the payment—"it's just another bill."

This overlap is perhaps most palpable in the case of formerly incarcerated people. Like anyone else, they are used to juggling a variety of debt obligations as they arise—medical and utility bills, housing rents, phone fees, credit card balances, and college loans, in addition to car notes and traffic fines. When caught in a squeeze, they are just as likely to borrow more money to make the most pressing payments. But as veterans of the criminal justice system, they are also more acutely aware of the need to balance risks against needs, especially in the period of reentry. While behind bars, their freedom dreams and peer conversations might have orbited around the allure of vehicles to be freshly acquired on release. Once on the outside, they find that negotiating over a new set of wheels, even when they can't really afford the car, is a snap compared to setting things straight with the DMV and obtaining or reclaiming a license, let alone finding a job and adequate housing. Knowing that high-status cars attract police scrutiny, especially when the driver and passengers are people of color, does not deter some of our interviewees from taking possession of them. They understand that the purchase of a BMW or a Benz may be a financial trap, skillfully manipulated by dealers and lenders, but the gratification it delivers is far superior to the other, mostly raw, deals on offer to the formerly incarcerated in low-income households. And some find that a dealer will only extend credit for high-end cars and not the lower-budget model they seek.

Should they be buying cars beyond their means? As in other instances of borrowing that overwhelmingly benefit the lender, we firmly believe that moral judgements should be reserved for the retailers and creditors. Sadly, consumer protections generally only apply when loan terms are found to be egregiously unfair, or when fraudulent methods have been deployed to get a quick sale on extortionate terms. But we believe these protections should automatically extend to situations in which a lender (in collusion with a dealer) is aware that borrowers can't pay. Marlon put it this way: "I personally think that they should be under the same rules as stock—the fiduciary rule with the stocks. If you know that the debt-to-income ratio is off, then they should not be pushing you to get a car—a car that has a payment that takes you out of that ratio." Surely it is no less predatory when a judge imposes fines and fees on defendants who cannot pay, thereby placing the state in the position of levying debt, ostensibly as a punishment, but invariably as a source of revenue?

From that angle we see a resemblance, if not an equivalence, between these two kinds of creditor and their respective courts of appeal. When it comes to enforcement of debt service, the differences are not so far apart on a spectrum. As we have pointed out, it is all too common through contempt of court to use the threat of detention to collect civil as well as state debts. The state is clearly more empowered as a creditor than a consumer lender would be. It has the capacity to mete out penalties which cannot be discharged, either in court or in bankruptcy, and which can lead directly to incarceration. But the forced status of American car ownership shapes and determines auto consumer debt to the point of minimizing its optional character. And for a significant portion of the population, this lack of volition is experienced as a real constraint, on a continuum with the unfreedom that inheres in the criminal justice system.

The widely noted movement of upper-income households back to urban centers over the last three decades has fueled enthusiasm for the car-free movement.[47] It has also meant that poverty is growing fastest in suburban parts of the US, where the challenge of reducing carbon emissions is most acute.[48] These population shifts are cyclical and by no means permanent; New York, for example, was losing some of its population before the much-ballyhooed pandemic flight of white- and no-collar households. But for the foreseeable future, high housing costs will likely continue to displace poorer families away from compact urban areas with ready access to public transit, and these are the people disproportionately snowed under by the cost of car ownership. The average household in the US spends as much as 17 percent of its total expenses on transportation, much more than for food.[49] But for low-income households, this burden is as high as 30 percent.[50] The larger problem is that more than half of all American households spend more than they earn.[51] For those held captive by that stark calculus, debt is the only way of making ends meet, and staying on the road.

Peer researchers Vincent Thompson (top) and Aiyuba Thomas (bottom), with their cars.

Chapter Five

Experiences—Chutes and Ladders

So if someone gets pulled over, they get police contact, it may just be a traffic violation then, but when they report to parole, parole will then tell them, "Well, you weren't supposed to operate a vehicle, or even possess a license without permission." Then they get thirty, ninety days in jail. Sometimes depending on your category, it could be up to a year. And at a time in somebody's life where they're just trying to rebuild it. You know, like thirty days is thirty days, but it could cost you the job that you had just gotten, or the apartment you had just managed to lease.

—Jamal

When Rhonda Jones walked out of federal prison after more than a dozen years inside, she had eighteen dollars to her name and a credit score in the basement. The thousands of hours she had spent working in the prison dining hall at a pay rate of twelve cents an hour didn't add up to much beyond covering the cost of her toothpaste and some of the phone calls she made to her children. Before her arrest, this African American mother of two had driven a BMW SUV. But the police had seized it, claiming it had been used for selling drugs, though none were ever found in the car. Rhonda was a powerhouse, she was organized, and she took the bull by the horns in tackling bureaucratic requirements. Shortly after her arrest, she had written to her creditor from jail, and included a photocopy of her indictment to prove that the car was now the property of the US government. The lender accepted this evidence and repossessed the car from the police lot, but her $8,000 deposit and four years of monthly car payments went down the tubes along with everything else she owned. After her release, while living in a Chicago halfway house as a condition of her parole, she had to make three separate trips to the DMV to reinstate her license. The long bus rides there and back, and the lengthy queues for each task she needed to accomplish, meant she could only complete a single piece of the necessary bureaucracy on each trip if she were to make it back to the halfway house for mandatory check-in.

After she obtained her license, a sister added her as a second driver to her car insurance policy. Now that she was licensed and insured, family members would lend her their cars so she could go on job interviews and to other appointments and errands. Rhonda knew that it took a toll on her sister; it "became a burden on her, really on the whole family" who sacrificed to share their cars, just so that she could reestablish her life. She also knew how fortunate she was to have family she could rely on, family who trusted her with their vehicles.

While she was incarcerated, some swindlers had applied for credit cards and other bills in Rhonda's name, and so there were collections agencies after her. On reentry, she obtained a letter of incarceration that specified her dates of arrest, incarceration, and release. She then provided copies to each of the three major credit bureaus, to prove that it was not she who had run up the debt. Some months later they issued her a new credit report, and her score had jumped to 700. Soon it was at 720, and then 750. Then, and only then, was she ready to buy a car.

Rhonda was by no means alone in discovering bogus debts, fees, and tickets in her name after a lengthy period of incarceration. Identity theft is a common problem for incarcerated people, whose conditions of capture make them easy prey—so much so that the Consumer Financial Protection Bureau has offered a "tip sheet" on "Protecting One's Credit While in the

Criminal Justice System."[1] Meanwhile, as Alexandra Natapoff found in her study of misdemeanors, anecdotal evidence suggests the DMV is chronically prone to error, though no one really knows how much. Natapoff was only able to locate a single study of DMV error rates—a "Florida legislative study [from 2000] of DMV insurance records that found error rates as high as 35 percent, leading to thousands of wrongful seizures."[2]

These errors can be costly. When La'Trice returned home to the Chicago area from Indiana state prison in 2016, she went to the DMV to reinstate her driver's license. There she learned it had been suspended over a 1999 ticket that she had failed to pay. "I'm like, in 1999 I was in prison. We did have a teddy-bear trolley there. I was like, did I get a ticket driving that?" But in the end, faced with the prospect of hiring a lawyer and going to court to challenge it, she just paid the $400 charge to settle the matter. Of course, not all traffic debt is bogus, but it is very difficult to shake off. As one of our peer researchers put it, "DMV don't go nowhere. You can do fifteen years and they are still going to be there."

As Rhonda pointed out, eighteen dollars is not a lot with which to rebuild your life. But many people emerge from prison without even that, and find themselves indebted to the DMV for ancient traffic fines about which they have no recollection, but which are now topped up with late penalties and other fees and fines. Besides, not everyone has Rhonda's savvy in matters of finance and bureaucratic procedure. Rhonda's parents had taught her from a young age about the importance of paying her bills on time and maintaining good credit. As a result, she understood the system well enough to know how much time and knowledge it took, and she had the wherewithal and tenacity to attend to complex and frustrating paperwork. But she was not alone in this disposition.

Several of the formerly incarcerated people with whom we spoke—all of them African American (but drawn from a class spectrum ranging from working poor to lower-middle class)—recalled how their parents had taught them the importance of paying bills on time, not borrowing more than they could afford, and maintaining good credit. This was a moral mindset as much as a practical one. LeMarcus recalled the lessons taught by the Jamaican-born aunt who raised him in Brooklyn: "She just tried to instill certain things, just certain things. That you always pay your debts, you always do what's right . . . If you tell somebody something, you give 'em your word, you always keep your word." This advice was dispensed along with practical guidance about financial literacy. Such skills are invaluable for those returning home from prison. The financial and bureaucratic challenge of rebuilding a life is formidable, and many inevitably wind up reliant on unscrupulous lenders as they attempt to do so. The credit system is opaque for a reason, and its manipulators prey upon transportation desperation and fantasy alike. In Rhonda's case, her efforts paid off. She got a seventy-two-month loan at 5.9 percent interest for a two-year-old Lexus and began driving for Uber. Others are not so fortunate.

Like most Americans, formerly incarcerated people usually purchase their cars on credit. In other words, the feeling of freedom is accompanied by the stress of indebtedness. Even if someone could save a few thousand dollars and/or borrow from family or friends for a down payment, it might not be enough to purchase a used car that was reliable. Those whose family members or friends had gifted them a car on its last legs upon their return home were enormously grateful. They knew it was crucial to their initial efforts to rebuild their lives. But they also struggled with the insecurity of relying on a car that could and did break down at inopportune moments and that was constantly needing costly repair. As soon as they were able, they made their way to a dealership for a loan on a more reliable vehicle.

Carceral geography, and its welter of fines, fees, and punishments, combines with the machinations of the auto loan and insurance industries to make car ownership something of a chutes and ladders game for many of those we interviewed. People invested significant amounts of scarce capital in their cars, but this was not necessarily a stable investment. The value of the car degraded as soon as it was driven, it could be destroyed in an accident, it could be repossessed by the creditor, or it could be seized by the state. It could also be the target of regressive extraction by the state through fees and fines.

That shiny icon of freedom lies nested within a web of debt and carcerality that extends across family and friends. This web functions as a second punishment on a broad swath of people. Someone who has "paid their debt to society" through enduring years in a cage now must pay again and again and again in cash. Unlike the penal sentence that is administered through the courts as a central source of judgment, this second punishment operates at the behest of profit-seeking beneficiaries, including local municipalities and state agencies. At worst it can lead to reincarceration, with people drawn back into illicit activity to stay ahead of their creditors or jailed as a consequence of debt collection. And this second punishment, like the first, extends far beyond the orbit of their own finances and well-being. Serving time takes a profound social, emotional, and economic toll on parents, children, spouses, partners, friends, and siblings of the person who is incarcerated. As that person returns home in debt to the state and with ruined credit, relatives and friends must offer both economic and practical support if the person is to succeed. As Rhonda put it, returning home from prison "is really, really hard. And if you don't have support [of family and friends], it's highly likely that you will return back to prison."

The License

Almost all our interviewees prioritized the reinstatement of their driver's license upon their release from prison. Most reported that it was more difficult to secure employment and housing without a license.[3] More importantly, they often needed to drive. But many had substantial outstanding DMV debt to pay before they could head to the window where they handed over the fees for a new license. One man from Queens, who was four months post-release after eight and a half years in prison, explained to us how incarceration and debt amplified each other. "Once you're incarcerated they are just going to keep adding on. So now you come home in a bunch of debt." He was earning $410 per week working in construction and had had to take out a $2,000 loan with interest to pay off his accumulated carceral debt, which included over $500 in DMV fines in addition to the cost of two old traffic tickets and more than $100 in fees for a permit and driver's test. He was forced to stay in a dormitory-style shelter because he could not find a landlord who would rent to him with his poor credit score. "Now I got all of this backed-up credit from before I went to jail and it's not going nowhere. So now I'm getting denied everywhere I go. I'm in shelter after shelter, I can't move around."

Among our interviewees, the cost to reinstate a license varied considerably, from a few hundred to a few thousand dollars. But even a few hundred dollars is a daunting sum for someone just returning from prison. Yet even after undertaking the lengthy, frustrating, and costly process of reinstatement, a record of license suspension still raises insurance premiums, and so the costs are cascading. One of our interviewees was given two speeding tickets in 2006 shortly before he was incarcerated for over a decade in New York State. On reentry, to reinstate his driver's license he had to pay $700 in fines in addition to the tickets. Now, even two years after his release, he continues to pay outsized insurance premiums because the lengthy license suspension is on his record. "I pay $314 a month . . . Because my license was suspended for so long and there was nothing I could do about it when I was in prison . . . Had I fixed it sooner, if I wasn't in jail, I wouldn't be going through that. My insurance would have probably been $120." Due to these high premiums, he could afford only limited coverage; full coverage would have been $500 per month, well beyond his means. As a result, the value of his car, his most significant asset, was not protected. By contrast, some interviewees told stories they had heard about people with full coverage who could not keep up with their car payments and had purposefully crashed their cars to use the insurance payment to avoid repossession and thereby protect their credit score. One man told us he had witnessed this tactic. "I'm at an auto body shop getting my car fixed, so I saw him—they was like planning it out. I guess they planned the whole joint out, and then right after I left they got into an accident. So I saw it like that too."

Some people emerged from prison with a stipulation that prevented them from reinstating their license for a set period. Until recently, many states automatically suspended licenses for at least six months for even minor drug offenses, in what were popularly termed "smoke a joint, lose your license" laws.[4] The Prison Policy Initiative reported that more than 190,000 licenses were suspended for non-driving drug offenses in 2016.[5] Campaigns to repeal these laws have been gaining ground, with only Arkansas, Alabama, and Florida holding out. This is a highly welcome development, but license suspension is still rife. The Free to Drive Campaign counts thirty-three states as well as the District of Columbia that "still suspend, revoke or refuse to renew driver's licenses for unpaid traffic, toll, misdemeanor and felony fines and fees."[6] License suspension is also a civil punishment leveraged by the state against parents (usually fathers) who are behind in child support payments.[7] A few of our interviewees returned from prison to discover they had driving stipulations or suspended licenses for reasons that were unclear to them. It's not surprising, then, that driving with a suspended license was reported to be a common, but necessarily risky, endeavor. In this respect, the formerly incarcerated join countless working poor Americans who simply cannot afford the fees necessary for a license reinstatement or have violations on their record for driving without insurance.

Lisa, a white woman in Indianapolis who had been out of prison for three years, had been active in a bipartisan coalition seeking to tackle this problem in Indiana, where an estimated 10 percent of drivers (some 330,000 in 2019) were on the road with a suspended license. As the Indiana Prosecuting Attorney's Office notes, most of those suspensions are for economic reasons—failure to pay fines and fees, or lack of car insurance.[8]

Lisa reminded us that such policies, which criminalize poverty, are irrational. A parent needs to drive to be able to earn the money required for child support. Given that driving is near mandatory, such a policy also means that many will drive without insurance, which then puts everyone on the road at risk of an uncompensated loss. This is not an issue in the dozen states with no-fault insurance systems. But in most states, coverage for injuries sustained in a collision with an uninsured motorist is an insurance add-on, and property damage for repair of one's vehicle is yet another add-on. Those who do not purchase these additional forms of coverage will have to shoulder any costs from such a collision themselves. And, of course, for those emerging from prison, such barriers to the means for gainful employment can force people into unlawful acts—either illegal driving and/or illicit earning—just when they are especially determined to stay within the rules.

In response to the pressure of reform advocates like Lisa, Indiana Governor Eric Holcomb signed House Bill 1199 into law in April 2021.[9] The new law does not affect the existing rules regarding license suspension for DUI, reckless driving, or moving violations. But it does have a provision that specifically targets nonviolent offenders returning from prison by waiving reinstatement fees for those who maintain employment or are enrolled in job training. This is a step in the right direction. But we would still question the logic that singles out violent offenders for continued economic extraction. They too have supposedly paid their "debt to society" by serving prison time, so why should they be liable for fees that the state acknowledges will impede their efforts to rebuild a law-abiding life?

Compulsory Consumption

People emerge from prison having lost whatever wheels they had at the time of their arrest, and in dire need of transportation. Depending on where they live, some are lucky and a subway or bus pass will do. Eric, who returned home to the Harlem apartment he shares with his wife, was happy to ride the subway to his new job, and then share his wife's car for their weekend outings to BJ's Wholesale in New Jersey or to visit family. He didn't want the expense or hassle of a car while he focused on rebuilding his life. Nor did one of our peer researchers, whose aunt welcomed him into her house in downtown Brooklyn, which was well served by the subway. In fact, car ownership in New York City tracks in inverse proportion to the density of public transportation. Eighty-three percent of households in Staten Island own a car, the only borough not connected to the subway, versus 22 percent in Manhattan.[10] But most people in the United States return from prison to places not well served by public transportation. One study by the Brookings Institution found that within US cities, "the typical job is only accessible to 27 percent of its metropolitan workforce by transit in 90 minutes or less."[11] In suburban and rural areas, the challenges are much greater. Peruse the crime blotter of any rural newspaper and you will find frequent listings of arrests for driving with a suspended license. For those coming home from prison, this barrier to access compounds the challenges they already face in securing stable employment and housing.

Those with supportive family and friends might be able to rely on them for rides, or borrow their cars, in order to get through the first few months while they find work and housing, and try to meet the requirements of the post-carceral bureaucracy. When Janiene, a white, college-educated woman in her mid-thirties left prison, her sister and brother-in-law welcomed her into their suburban Indianapolis home. They gifted her their old station wagon, which was on its last legs. She drove it for a few months before it finally died for good, and she found herself sheltering by the side of the highway waiting for a tow truck as cars raced by at seventy-five miles an hour. Her family paid for the tow. The gifted car had been a lifeline. With it, Janiene managed to find a decent job as a manager in a small business, where she was doing well. Her work was an easy drive from her sister's place but would have been a two-and-a-half-hour bus ride each way.

Having a car meant she could stay late at work or fill in at the last minute, as she often did, becoming a highly valued employee in the process. For the first two days after the car broke down, her retired stepfather drove over a half hour across town to collect her and then another thirty minutes to her job. At the end of the day, he did that in reverse. Janiene was grateful but knew the arrangement was unsustainable. "Even though I had support of family, it was not practical to expect them to get me to that job, where it was nowhere close to where they lived." It was time for her to buy a car.

Janiene realized that any vehicle she could afford outright would be unreliable, require costly repairs, and possibly be unsafe. So as soon as she had a day off, she headed to Drive Time, a used-car franchise chain. She had Googled a bunch of places, but knew her options were constrained. Her car had been repossessed when she was incarcerated, and, with that on her record, her credit was shot until she could rebuild it. Drive Time had TV and radio spots advertising their willingness to approve almost anyone. She knew that would mean a high interest rate, but at least they had a decent selection of cars. A friend loaned her $600, to which she added the $600 she had managed to save, to make the down payment. She drove off the lot in a Mazda Sport with a sticker price of $11,000 and a seventy-two-month loan at approximately 17 percent for which she would have to dish out $342 a month. At that rate, six years later she would have paid $26,000 for a car originally priced at less than half that amount. The car dealership set up insurance as part of the finance package. It too was calibrated to her credit history, and after eight years in prison she had no recent driving record, so her insurance premiums were steep. As she told us, "I realize there's incentives and all that, they're not just being helpful, but you don't have time to shop around. I just wanted to get it taken care of, so of course I ended up paying more in insurance." Fortunately, within two years and through a determined effort she had rebuilt her credit history and was able to refinance the loan for only 3.5 percent. But, as she put it, "my credit would not be going up if I did not have the necessary means to be able to get and maintain employment." A job requires a car and vice versa, and in the meantime a record of incarceration continues to exact a financial toll.

Janiene felt fortunate and grateful for the support she received from family and friends. Lacking any assets, and a recent credit history or decent credit score, she and others like her had to rely on friends and family to help them purchase their vehicles. But there are many others who come from households and social networks that are already economically over-whelmed. They might have to cosign loans for one another, but their credit risks are shared if they do so. One survey found that 38 percent of US cosigners (including auto loans, student loans, and credit cards) ended up paying some portion of the loan in question, and that credit scores subse-quently dropped for 28 percent of cosigners, because the primary borrower was late to pay or failed to make a payment.[12]

When LeMarcus first came home from prison to Brooklyn, his friends and family pooled their resources to make sure he had some money to get himself started. He had enough for a down payment, but when he went to a car dealer he learned his credit was "too messed up" to secure a loan. He would need someone to cosign. Though his friends and family had been generous with money, it was hard to find someone willing and able to put the car in their name. Finally, a woman he was dating agreed to do so, and while her credit was better than his, it still wasn't great. They went to AutoExpo, a dealership on Long Island that had an agreement with Santander Bank and was willing to loan to subprime borrowers. The lot was full of BMWs and Mercedes. LeMarcus had wanted a Honda, or "some kind of regular car," but wound up with a Mercedes, since that was the only vehicle for which they were offered a loan. He knew this was a bad deal because he didn't want a car that would cost so much to maintain. But the bank financing Hondas "wanted a more solid foundation, good credit, and a higher income. So it was actually harder to get that car." When we joked that his Mercedes was much cooler than a Honda, he rebuked us that this was of little comfort. He rued the fact that had he been able to maintain his credit—as he had done before being incarcerated—he could have purchased a less-expensive car with lower interest and insurance payments.

In the end, LeMarcus put down $5,000 for the car and approximately $900 for insurance. His monthly payment was $800 per month, and his insurance bill an additional $500: a whopping $1,300 per month before gas, parking, or repairs. Ironically, we found that many people newly released from prison could end up driving the status car of their dreams precisely *because* their subprime credit score puts them at the mercy of rapacious lenders. How long they can hold on to those cars is another matter entirely. When the Mercedes gets repossessed, the chance of acquiring a Honda becomes even slimmer. And if a cosigned car like LeMarcus's gets repossessed, that's two credit scores shot.

A shiny new car is sold as a ladder to the good life, but it can all too easily become a chute down into deeper poverty. While some people had purchased cars at auction for relatively modest sums, others had bought those listed at well over $20,000 through opaque financing contracts. Car payments of around $500 a month were common among our interviewees, though some were considerably higher. These were more or less in line with national trends. According to Experian, the average monthly payment on a new car in 2021 was $568, and for a used car, $397. But for many formerly incarcerated owners, their attempts to climb the ladder ended with an unwanted visit from the repo man.

One Brooklyn man had his car repossessed after years of payments when there was only $8,000 left on his loan. In a conversation among peer researchers, Zach Gillespie recalled the routine of the repo man who trolled his old Harlem neighborhood. "There used to be a Crown Victoria, and there used to be a dude, and he wore a green shirt. He had a gun. I was like, dude is with a gun and they're not cops. But they come out early in the morning, like early, early, like I'm talking about like five o'clock in the morning." Repossession was a looming threat. Another peer researcher recalled "a couple of people [I knew] that went through repossession. I also know people who just gave up like, no I ain't paying this. So they just parked their car maybe two blocks away, they just don't park it at their house."

The High-Wire Act

Post-incarceration is a high-wire act because people are trying to balance their simultaneous and pressing needs for housing, transportation, and gainful employment. The balancing feat looks a lot different depending on the location. Many of our interviewees lived outside of New York City, and most paid several hundred dollars a month in rent, in addition to several hundred on their car payments and insurance. Rent was usually a few hundred dollars more than the car, but not always. This was tight, but maybe doable. For those who lived in New York City, the high price of housing in some neighborhoods was offset by the availability of public transportation, but those locations were out of reach for most, unless they were returning to live with a spouse or other relatives in an established home. The average monthly price for a studio apartment in Corona, Queens (one of the least expensive neighborhoods in the city) is $1,400 a month. That may compare favorably to hipster Williamsburg, Brooklyn, where the average price for a studio is more than twice as much—but it is almost two and a half times more than the rents on a one- or two-bedroom townhouse apartment in Indianapolis, where some of our other interviewees resided.

Decades of gentrification have pushed many low-income New Yorkers into neighborhoods in the outer boroughs or first-ring suburbs that are chronically underserved by public transportation. Jose Diaz, a member of our research team, was originally from a predominately Latinx neighborhood of Brooklyn served by several subway lines. Upon release after more than a decade in upstate prisons, he found himself priced out of his now rapidly gentrifying home neighborhood. He eventually secured a room in

Staten Island. After the first few months of commuting by ferry and bus for well over two hours each way, he purchased a car.

Other peer researchers in the city confirmed that it is much "harder to get an apartment than a car." As one of them explained: "Compare a car to an apartment. It don't cost no money for you to get into a $100,000 car. But for you to get into a one-bedroom apartment or studio or even a basement apartment, you probably got to pay $1,500 times three, you got to at least pay $5,000 because you know they got the broker's fees and all that." He spoke from experience. When he returned home to Queens after more than a decade in prison, he spent months apartment hunting while sleeping on a relative's couch. But when he went to purchase a car, it was smooth sailing. "Once you come in and say you want a car, they kind of just do everything for you to put you in the car as long as you have a little down payment. With this apartment? I need to see a job, I need to get references, you have to have money up front, you have to look at bank statements—there's mad things they have to go through. Anybody could get a car. Anybody can't just get an apartment."

As a result, there were some people for whom an apartment was so far out of reach that they focused on the car instead. A status car could hide the fact that an adult man was still living with his mother or in a shelter. It could conceal the fact that the driver was actually indebted at more than twice the value of the automobile. But it was really only those who lived in neighborhoods well served by public transportation who were able to avoid loans altogether. Marlon, a first-generation Nigerian American man, returned from prison in 2018 to the house in Brooklyn where he had grown up. He had no rent to pay, but he gave his mother several hundred dollars each month to help with the household expenses. Some months after his return, he enrolled in community college and found a stable job. When Marlon went to purchase a car, he chose one in the lot that was priced at $23,000 and told the salesman he was prepared to put $5,000 down. He had more saved, but he wanted to hear the terms offered before upping his deposit. He thought, "Okay, the car is $23,000, I am putting down $5,000 so that will leave $18,000 to finance."

Marlon had been left waiting in an office, and when he went to see what was taking the salesman so long, he could hear a colleague telling him to just "hurry up and get him to sign the paperwork. Just hurry up and get him to sign." But then, as he looked at the computer screen in front of the salesman, he saw he was being set up to pay $17,000 in interest over seven years. "I said 'I'm good, I don't need this.' Like—I left that place, like y'all crazy, what y'all think I am?" The high interest—nearly equaling the sticker price of the car—wasn't the only scam: "They tell you they need to package in for some tire and wheel package, they tell you got to pay a dealer fee and the taxes, and it all comes out to $10,000." Marlon was good with numbers, and he also was primed to see the scam. His cousin had lost his car to repossession this way, and had his credit shot. So he walked away, and decided to rent when he needed to drive instead of buying, at least until he could buy on better terms.

Marlon knew he was lucky in this regard. He knew how many men coming home from prison relied on their female relatives and partners to help house them. When we spoke, he had just read Matthew Desmond's book *Evicted*, and summed up the gendered collision of carceral geography and racial capitalism: "Men go to prison; women get evicted." These two might collide as they did for Laquan. He had grown up in the same Brooklyn neighborhood as Marlon, but he couldn't return home. His mother had lost her house when she could not keep up with the mortgage payments.

Cascading Costs of Police Contact

Flashing blue lights in the rearview mirror are costly for justice-involved people in ways that far exceed the ostensible purpose of the traffic and penal codes. The financial consequence of police contact can vary greatly. While being pulled over usually meant the price of tickets, fines, and potentially the ballooning costs of arrest, a number of our interviewees recounted stories of corrupt police who solicited bribes or stole money or drugs from them. They might have been pulled over for speeding, and then, if they were driving a nice car or were well-dressed, the police officer began to insinuate that they must have some money on them. Black and brown drivers who are solicited in this way no doubt recognize that refusal to hand over the kickback might entail bigger risks than complying. One woman reported having drugs planted in her car, a practice that has been widely documented.[13] But just as common were stories from those who claim they were pulled over, searched, and defrauded. If marijuana was found, the police took both the drugs and whatever money the driver had on them and let them go. Or they might be arrested, but at their booking the arresting officer reported they had far less cash on them when they were seized, and so presumably had pocketed the difference.

An arrest sets in motion a process of cascading financial harm. This secondary punishment is enforced regardless of whether arrestees are innocent or guilty of the charge in question. The court system is so backlogged that those who cannot afford bail might linger in jail for months or even years before trial, losing their jobs, homes, and cars in the process. But even if the person has committed the offense, the financial injury can dwarf the infraction in ways that are prohibitive (and unconstitutional). The outcome can make their "debt to society" both unpayable and inescapable.

Consider peer researcher Vincent Thompson, who while still on parole was pulled over for a search on the pretext of a low-pressure tire, and subsequently reincarcerated. When we visited him in jail as he awaited a transfer to an upstate facility, he was bereft and digging deep for the determination necessary to weather the outsized consequences of a minor mistake. The reincarceration resulted in his eviction. His landlord had Vincent's possessions dumped on the curb, where they were taken or destroyed. He lost the $1,500 security deposit he had scraped together for the down payment on the apartment. The eviction marred his rental record and would make it nearly impossible to obtain a new lease. He also borrowed several thousand dollars from his girlfriend for a lawyer to fight the charge, and lost his internship and the monthly stipend that it paid, as well as the deposit and two months of payments on his car. Eight months later, when Vincent was released, he had to start all over again. A tiny amount of marijuana—a substance that was in the process of being decriminalized in New York when he was pulled over—had ended up costing him and his girlfriend well over $10,000 in addition to eight months of his life.

The punitive impact of a car arrest can reveal how the costs of racial capitalism and those of American carcerality are borne by family, friends, and a wider community. For example, Hassan, an African American man from Long Island, told one peer researcher that he was working a good job and had purchased a new $40,000 car. He was making payments of $500 a month when he was pulled over while driving and arrested for possession of 1.2 grams of cocaine. This small amount is only a fifth-degree possession charge, but upon his arrest Nassau County, Long Island, officials seized the car and wanted to sell it. There was a lien on it from the bank, and so a lengthy struggle ensued over the vehicle. Eventually the bank won out and retook possession, but not before they had made several thousand dollars billing Hassan's wife for months of car payments on a vehicle they knew was in the county's possession.

We heard countless other stories of how the financial stress of incarceration washes over families. Steve felt bad about the heavy burden his incarceration put on his family. "On top of lawyers, on top of commissary," on top of the stress of having their loved one in jail—there were the costs generated by the car.[14] He was nineteen years old and his grandmother had helped him lease a BMW, which he was driving at the time he was arrested. The police held the car for six months, during which time his family kept up payments on the lease even though they could not access the vehicle. Eventually, his father had to pay a lawyer to break the lease. This prompted the auto dealer to retrieve their car from the police. In the end, in addition to the thousands it cost to hire the lawyer, his grandmother's credit score took a dive and his family had paid over $2,000 on a lease for a vehicle they could not access.

Police contact can be expensive even if it doesn't result in an arrest. Tickets and fees that may make little difference to wealthy drivers can be devastating to households on very tight budgets. The geography of the carceral system extends families and other key relationships from urban neighborhoods through rural prisons, necessitating additional burdens that involve car travel. New York State, for example, has fifty-four correctional facilities, but no medium or maximum facility within the New York City regional hub. This means that 58 percent of incarcerated persons from New York City are housed in prisons more than two hundred miles from home.[15] Most of these facilities are not served by public transportation, and the monthly bus system that had been maintained for families was eliminated in a 2011 budget cut. Simply visiting someone in prison requires access to a car. For children to see their parents, or for siblings, spouses, or partners to see one another can entail driving while Black through predominantly white rural communities. One man felt awful about the speeding tickets his sister racked up "coming to see me like eight hours away, trying to make it there in time" for his facility's limited visiting hours.

Climbing Back Up the Ladder

Arrest is not the only pathway to this downward spiral of harm and loss. Formerly incarcerated people are navigating many of the same linked challenges as other low-income Americans, desperately trying to balance the costs of housing, transportation, health care, and other needs. Like them, they are living one unlucky break from a fall down the chute. But the costly impact of their incarceration—with its attendant damaged credit, fees and fines, and loss of assets—also erodes any scarce resources they might have to surmount these challenges. From the bottom of the chute they must try to climb back up the ladder. La'Trice, who had joked about getting a ticket for driving the teddy-bear trolley in prison, wound up deep in medical debt a few years after her release. She is far from alone—a recent study estimated that 17.8 percent of Americans have medical debt in the hands of collections agencies.[16] Her medical bills triggered a financial collapse that would result in the repossession of her car.

La'Trice had just turned fifty when we spoke, and was a remarkably good-natured person. She saw her upbeat attitude as a necessary resource in life, and a result of being buoyed by her late mother's loving voice inside her head. When she first came home after two decades in state prison, she found that "mentally, the criminal record stopped me more than anything." She dreaded having to explain it to a potential employer and, as a result, at first only applied for minimum wage jobs (which paid $7.25) despite her skills and college education. It was her mom who helped her get out of this mindset, who told her to stop beating herself up and just put herself out there. With her mom's encouragement and the support of her sister and friends, she did just that and slowly rebuilt her life after prison. She weathered the halfway house, and an awful experience of a mugging at the bus stop where she had to wait in the dark after she finished her late shift. She had paid the bogus $400 charge at the DMV, reinstated her license, was working two jobs she liked and excelling at them. She was renting a condo in Indianapolis and driving a newer Ford compact model purchased at CarMax when she got sick.

Being financially upended by illness is a common story in the US. In fact, medical debt is the nation's leading cause of bankruptcy. But it is also an unsurprising fate for someone who endured many years in the US prison system, with its poor-quality health care, substandard food, decrepit and potentially toxic facilities, and conditions of extreme stress and violence. On reentry, La'Trice needed surgery. After her recovery, she kept her full-time desk job, which only paid ten dollars an hour. But she had to leave her second part-time job, even though it paid more (twelve dollars per hour) because it was too physically demanding. Even though she had health insurance, she nonetheless faced huge medical bills which began to pile up alongside her outstanding student loan. Finally, like so many Americans, a bout of illness and associated medical debt forced her into bankruptcy. When we spoke with her she was in the process of rebuilding her credit.

La'Trice had never missed a car payment, but the car was nonetheless lost in the bankruptcy and the repo men came to collect it. She had bought it at CarMax, a big dealership, and knew her payments were on the high side. But this was her first car on reentry and, with only $450 in cash to put down, she was at the mercy of the lender. The Ford was listed at $14,000 and her monthly payments were $469. She was two years into a six-year contract. We asked her to estimate how much she had paid for the vehicle before it was repossessed.

She worked out the numbers. "Let's do a little calculation . . . So wait a minute, so we're looking at four hundred and sixty-nine dollars times twenty-four . . . " Then La'Trice did a double-take. "That can't be right. Four hundred and—I'm trying to calculate here, my brain is not working very well. It looks like I paid like roughly eleven thousand dollars on that car! But that can't be." We took out our phones to double-check her math. But yes, it was true. Including the $450 she put down, she had already paid $11,706 for the car before it was repossessed, plus the money for repairs and maintenance she had put into it, including over $300 she'd spent on new tires shortly before it was taken back. We all agreed that someone at CarMax was happy. La'Trice on the other hand was not. "Now I'm gonna cry. Look at what you made me do," she half-joked. "That car was not worth that!" To put her $469 monthly car payment into perspective, we observed that she was paying $560 a month for her apartment. By the time she paid for insurance, gas, parking, and repairs, she was spending much more on transportation than housing.

After paying $1,900 to a lawyer to file the bankruptcy, La'Trice began climbing the ladder again. *Again.* She found a job that came with Blue Cross/ Blue Shield insurance—a far better policy than her previous one. Finally, she would have some portion of her $400 prescription lenses covered. Finally, she would only have to make a small co-pay of $10 a month for her daily medications. She bought another car, this time an SUV. La'Trice had to hunt for a dealership that would lend to someone with a bankruptcy on their record, but in the end she actually found a more reputable dealer than CarMax and got better terms on the loan. She had been able to save $1,500 to put down on it and was now paying $352 a month—over $100 less per month than the Ford had cost, and that had been a compact car. When we spoke, she was getting ready to refinance now that her credit score was rising thanks to her careful planning.

The ladder out of prison is not the upward path powered by hard work and self-discipline mythologized in the American dream. Steady toil, patience, fortitude, and even optimism may be necessary. The support of family and friends can make a difference. So can a reliable car. But the journey is still fraught at every rung. The profit systems of carcerality and creditocracy are constantly exerting pressure, amplified, as always, by the uneven rituals of American racism. Together they operate as a powerful drag, thwarting even the most strenuous efforts to climb.

Your car is spying on you.

Chapter 6

Carceral Creep Meets
Surveillance Capitalism

We feel like all data is credit data. We just don't know how to use it yet.
—Douglas Merrill, CEO of Zest Financial

Several of our interviewees emerged from long prison sentences to find that twenty-first-century cars host a dizzying array of new technological features. Among other things, they have become enormous mobile computers. The new smart car is a key node in the emergent culture of hyper-surveillance and data extraction—a technological frontier where, in the words of sociologist Ruha Benjamin, "the sticky web of carcerality extends even further, into the everyday lives of those who are purportedly free."[1] Through our interviews, we were able to glimpse just how far beyond the gates of the prison or county jail the tentacles of carceral capitalism have crept. As automobile-surveillance systems are engineered to capture any data that can be bought or sold, every driver is dragged into the data marketplace, like it or not. For those already socially disadvantaged, the effects are compounded. Data-driven policies in commerce, education, and governance are routinely promoted as if they are empirical and objective, and therefore as welcome correctives to the human biases that allow both credit and carceral systems to operate as manifestations of American structural racism and classism. Yet in practice, because of how the technologies are employed, designed, and operated, they often serve instead to further the violence of these systems. As Kwame, a formerly incarcerated African American man in Indianapolis, put it, "I don't mind technology. It's all about who is controlling it though."

Returning after a long stretch in prison means contending with the rapid technological developments that happened during your absence. Email, smartphones, online portals, and requisite apps all present a potential Rip van Winkle experience for people who must adapt to new technologies that are taken for granted and utilized by everyone from state agencies to potential employers. Jayden, a middle-aged African American man who had grown up in North Carolina before moving to New York in his early twenties, was one of our very first interviewees. His father had taught him to fix cars when he was growing up down South and he had worked in an auto shop and also done repairs for friends in the alley next to his apartment. But when he returned home in 2016 after seventeen years in New York State prisons, cars had changed. Even a ten-year-old vehicle was now so thoroughly computerized that he felt disoriented when he opened the hood.

Car repair now requires the purchase of expensive software packages and the knowledge to use them. But the more superficial, and obvious, changes—automobiles that come without keys, are loaded with rear cameras or Global Positioning Systems, and have outlets for smartphone connection—make it relatively easy and even pleasurable for most drivers returning to the road after the brutal experience of years of enforced stasis. Even those like Jayden, who are used to fixing up their vehicles, are probably unaware of the extent to which the computerization of their cars is a ground zero for the ever-expanding web of data where finance, surveillance, and carcerality meet. Most do not realize how the digital upgrades and accessories that offer a more comfortable and exciting ride are also new modes of discipline and extraction. They do not suspect that, even as they are driving to the job needed to pay off their automobile loan, a new profit source has opened—tracking the microphysics of their vehicle use and selling that data back to the credit agency, the insurance company, and the police.

Surveillance

There are vital ecological and traffic-safety reasons for the authorities to keep an eye on the road. But much of this surveillance is instead undertaken to track and control racialized and poor populations and/or to extract wealth through revenue policing. Road surveillance has a deeply racialized history, from the slave patrol to the sundown town to the roadblocks deployed by US border patrol. And for many female drivers, the experience of having their car followed to their home or workplace evokes fears of being stalked. Renee Johnson, a formerly incarcerated African American woman, recounted for us the many times she had been pulled over by Indianapolis police for driving while Black. Her car had been searched repeatedly, despite the extra care she took to obey the traffic laws and keep the vehicle in good working order. After securing a well-paid job at a pharmaceutical firm she moved to another neighborhood, renting an apartment in Speedway—a predominantly white area near the Indianapolis Speedway. Her very presence there as one of the few Black residents drew police attention, and she found herself pulled over multiple times by officers; "and they were white men, each and every time" who "seemed affronted by the fact that I could live in Speedway."

On one occasion, a patrol car followed her home; "I mean, watching me park my car, get my groceries out. They literally watched me put my key in my door before they would drive away." The experience was terrifying. "I felt like something was going to happen to me, by the police, who were following me home," she recalled. "I've never been followed home in that way by anybody ... Sort of like a stalker, or some man who's trying to, like, potentially assault you or violate you. I felt that from the police. Following me home, that slow crawl with their car, and the lights out." Inside her home, heart pounding, she found herself peeking out the window to see if they would drive off. Even from behind the locked door she said that she no longer felt safe. The police had sent her a message. They knew where she lived; they could mess with her if they wanted.

But road surveillance extends far beyond the profound problem of police targeting Black motorists by sight. Jeff Williams knew he was insulated by his whiteness when he drove through Indianapolis to work or to visit the museum on his day off. He enjoyed driving in the city; it approximated that feeling of freedom he had dreamed of while in prison. But even in his almost entirely white, central Indiana hometown of twenty thousand, he felt watched by the police, who regularly pulled people over, including himself and members of his family and neighbors, for "driving while poor." Incarcerated at seventeen, he only got his license after being released, and by then was in his mid-twenties. Like Renee, he took great care to obey the traffic laws and to keep his affairs in order. When the police ran his plates, they knew he had been convicted of a felony. No matter that it was ten years in his past. They came out of the cruiser, "hand on their gun . . . thinking that you're about to do some crazy stuff just because you have committed a felony once in your life." It was scary. "I don't want a cop running my plates or being behind me at all. It makes me very nervous."

When Renee and Jeff handed their license to a police officer, they knew they were turning over a master key to all sorts of information. When the cops "run the license" through the computer in their car, they are connected to the DMV and local police records. In some states they are also automatically connected to the National Crime Information Center database, which hosts at least fourteen different lists—including the gang file, the supervised release file, the sex offender registry, and state and federal police records that constitute the rap sheet. In other states, the ability to make this connection is not automatic, but can only be approved through a formal request process. As numerous studies and lawsuits have revealed, these databases are both racially biased and error-prone.[2] The computerization of automobile-based surveillance does not resolve fundamental problems of bureaucratic error and racial bias, and so it can end up intensifying the criminalization of poverty.

While all drivers rightly must undertake an exam that establishes their basic competence behind the wheel and knowledge of traffic rules, Renee and Jeff also understood that the driver's license is utilized as a tool to discipline people for financial behavior that has little to do with maintaining traffic safety. Jeff's brother had been stuck for two years with a suspended license. He simply could not afford the $1,500 reinstatement fees. He had no DUIs or other dangerous driving infractions but had gotten behind in payments for traffic fines, and the late penalties began to add up. A neighbor of his was jailed for nine months for repeatedly driving with a suspended license. "No one got harmed, no one got robbed, it's just crazy to me." The absolute necessity of owning a car in most of the US forces these drivers to make the difficult choice between loss of employment and extreme financial hardship or breaking the law by driving with a suspended license.

Armed Debt Collectors

As seen in previous chapters, license reinstatement is a priority for many returning home from prison, some because their license to drive lapsed during their time inside, or had been suspended or revoked as part of their sentence. Others had to pay off debt from fines and fees. The rules for license suspension and revocation differ by state and have changed over time. For obvious reasons, a record of dangerous driving can result in suspension in the interest of public safety. For example, for a first offense of driving under the influence of alcohol or drugs, New York State will revoke a license for at least one year, while in Texas the license is suspended for ninety days and a temporary driving permit is issued for the first forty of those days.[3]

But all states have statutes that allow for at least some license suspension for *non-driving* offenses. Some of these penalties are meant to deter or punish. For example, Nevada suspends licenses for those convicted of graffiti spraying, and, as we noted earlier, the federal government has pressured and incentivized states to suspend licenses for drug-related convictions. But many of these policies are purely extractive, or they are used to strong-arm debtors to pay up. For example, several states suspend licenses for unpaid taxes, though the threshold for suspension differs: Louisiana suspends the license for tax arrears of $1,000 or more, while New York suspends for sums of $10,000 or higher.[4] In Ohio, failure to appear in court or to pay a court fine for a first-, second-, third-, or fourth-degree misdemeanor charge results in license suspension.[5] South Dakota will suspend a license for all unpaid state debt, including delinquent student loans.[6]

These techniques both criminalize and profit from poverty on a massive scale, turning the driver's license "into a form of collateral" for state debt.[7] In 2015, some 900,000 licenses were under suspension in the state of Virginia simply for unpaid court costs or fines.[8] While wealthier drivers can easily afford to pay fines or fees they accrue, the working poor are forced into the same situation as Jeff's brother. Drive without a license and risk being incarcerated, or stop driving and lose their job.

In addition, most states suspend the licenses of non-custodial parents who fail to pay mandated child support. Among our interviewees were fathers who had to pay off thousands of dollars in child support penalties accrued during incarceration before they could apply for license reinstatement. This is akin to using the license for collecting federal student loans, court fees, or traffic fines. The child-support license suspension policy is motivated by a similar dedication to debt recovery by states. Temporary Assistance for Needy Families (TANF) recipients are also forced to sign their child support rights over to the state.[9] Contrary to the semantics of the term "child support," this means that most of the payments collected through license suspension do not actually go to the child, they are harvested directly by state governments. Of course, wealthier parents also fall behind in court-mandated child support, which is paid directly to the custodial parent. But they are more likely to be able to make up the back payments and/or can afford legal counsel to assist in structuring a viable payment plan before their license is held.

Child support policy is one of the many channels through which the DMV has been pulled into the dragnet of surveillance and carcerality. Child Support Enforcement (CSE) federal legislation enacted in 1975 compelled custodial parents (usually mothers) to provide the social security numbers of non-custodial parents for tracking purposes. Under the Clinton administration the practice of tracking mushroomed and, almost inevitably, became interlinked with DMV databases. The 1994 Crime Bill, controversial for turbo-boosting mass incarceration, birthed other databanks like the sex-offender registries and the notoriously flawed gang databases that facilitated overzealous, racialized policing of Black and brown youth.[10] The equally contentious welfare reform bill of 1996 (the Personal Responsibility and Work Opportunity Reconciliation Act) came close on its heels. This new policy helped states establish computerized, data-rich child support enforcement registries, and mandated that "all state and federal child support agencies must have access to the motor vehicle and law enforcement locator systems of all states."[11] It further dictated that states have the authority to suspend licenses for overdue child support.[12] In worst-case scenarios, the law has led to reincarceration for driving with a suspended license as working-poor parents navigate the near-impossible bind between clearing their child support debt and the need to drive to earn income to pay it off.

Carceral Capitalism Meets the (Faulty) Algorithm

In the quarter century since these kinds of interlinkage were mandated, computational power and speed have accelerated beyond recognition. In the wake of 9/11, new modes of surveillance and carceral entrapment have proliferated and became normalized including, notably, the expansion of racial profiling policies to target Muslim, Arab, and Middle Eastern persons. The introduction of the Real ID in 2005 transformed the driver's license into a de facto national identity card, affording even broader federal scrutiny and control over movements and activities. In this new climate of escalating surveillance, both the FBI and ICE have made extensive use of their unmonitored access to DMV data.[13] Both agencies have availed themselves of the use of facial-recognition software that crossmatches images captured by surveillance cameras with the massive databases holding driver's license images. These images, in turn, are tied to home addresses, vehicle registration numbers, and driving records. In addition to triggering fundamental privacy concerns about how this software is used to track attendance at, say, political or religious gatherings, the facial recognition algorithms are error-prone and racially and gender biased. Investigations show much higher rates of false identification for photos of darker-skinned men and women than for white men. Thus, the risks of being falsely identified and accused are maldistributed.[14] Bear in mind that for those who lack funds for effective counsel, a false accusation can easily result in a plea deal, incarceration, and cascading debt.

Facial-recognition software is only one of the ways by which drivers' data is now collected, amplified, and utilized for surveillance by the authorities. Over the past decade and a half, police departments across the country have been encouraged to invest in automated license plate reader technology (ALPR). In 2021 alone, the Department of Homeland Security granted more than $50 million to law enforcement agencies to support the purchase of ALPR systems.[15] These cameras, which can be installed on police cruisers or placed at fixed street locations, have the capacity to capture thousands of license plates per minute. The plate number is bundled with the time, date, and location where it was spotted, along with a photograph of the vehicle—and potentially the people inside it. The scans are automatically fed into software systems that cross-reference them and look for a match against a "hot list" of license plates. These lists are routinely compiled by law enforcement or other state or federal agencies, and they combine information from multiple databases. Any jurisdiction or private entity with an ALPR system can have it uploaded with multiple hot lists or compile its own.[16]

Hot lists might include license plate numbers for vehicles reported as stolen, named in Amber alerts, or with expired registration; the numbers on the lists are also associated with registered sex offenders, parolees, those on terrorist watch lists or gang member databases, or other persons of interest to the compiler.[17] This data is archived, and some agencies dispose of it after a set period ranging from a few months to a few years. But many hold on to it indefinitely, resulting in a web of databases storing billions of time-stamped locations.[18] Algorithms can be used to establish geographic patterns or to identify plates associated with an area of interest.[19]

A study by the nonprofit Electronic Frontier Foundation (EFF) on the use of such technology in California found that only .05 percent of the billions of scans matched to a hot list.[20] This leaves most "innocent" cars nonetheless surveilled and their movements archived, whether they have been recorded in the parking lot of a mosque,[21] a doctor's office, a strip club, or near a political rally, raising major privacy concerns that account for why at least some states have decided to put limits on the use of ALPRs.[22] Meanwhile, ALPR data is prone to significant margins of error. According to the CEO of a company that pools ALPR data for law enforcement, "between 1% and 10% of license plate hits are misreads, depending on the system."[23] This is far lower than the results of a randomized control study cited by NYU's Brennan Center, which found error rates of 37 percent for fixed readers (i.e., attached to a building or light pole) and 35 percent for mobile ALPRs.[24] Mistakes can have hazardous consequences. In 2020, police officers forced a Black mother and her children to lay facedown on the pavement of a Colorado shopping mall, handcuffed and at gunpoint, because their license plate reader mistook her car for a stolen motorcycle from another state.[25]

Police and other state agencies purchase the ALPR technology from private vendors including Vigilant Solutions, with which ICE signed a $6.1 million contract in 2018.[26] Vigilant, which also markets facial-recognition systems, promotes the technology to municipalities in part by pointing to its value in revenue policing. In 2016, Vigilant undertook a pilot program to market its product, giving the cameras to local law enforcement agencies for free. But they tacked a 25 percent processing fee on top of the tickets and court fees and fines collected, which were to be paid directly to Vigilant under threat of arrest.[27] As the EFF, the ACLU, and other civil rights advocates have noted, this further incentivizes police to essentially become armed debt collectors and data miners for their jurisdiction.[28] Jeff told us that, for the police in his Indiana town, "that's like their main thing, that's what they do mainly in this town, is ride around and read plates." A car associated with a driver whose license has been suspended for unpaid state debt can be on a hot list simply because of the suspension. This is a pretext for a traffic stop, an additional ticket, a surcharge for the ALPR technology, and the potential threat of incarceration.[29]

Vigilant and other surveillance companies, like Flock Safety, market their ALPR technology to homeowner and neighborhood associations, as well as to malls, shopping centers, office parks, apartment complexes, and other sites whose owners can then elect to share their data directly with local law enforcement. Vigilant's sister company, DRN (Digital Recognition Network), markets the technology to insurance companies, debt collectors, and lenders.[30] Both firms further incentivize the repossession industry to add to their databases by paying repo men for scans. By 2019, Vigilant and DRN had amassed over nine billion scans, allowing for sophisticated algorithmic tracking of individual vehicles over time. As many of our interviewees affirmed, if the car is an exoskeleton (with a unique external frame), the technology allows its users a "highly accurate digital dossier of the sum total of a person's movements over time."[31] Vigilant claims that, while privately collected data in its database is shared with law enforcement, law enforcement data is not shared with private clients.[32] Whether or not this is true, it is clear that the data represents Vigilant's core asset. The more it collects and archives, the more value its tools generate both for itself and its clients.

Thankfully, there are some legal limits to the overreach of the DMV. The 1994 Driver's Privacy Protection Act was drafted in response to a high-profile, fatal case of stalking, in which actress Rebecca Schaeffer was murdered by a man who obtained her address through a private investigator who had access to DMV data. The law prohibits the DMV from sharing personal information "derived from an individual's motor vehicle records to anyone other than that individual." But there are many exceptions to this rule. The legislation allows for the sharing of data with state and federal agencies as well as for the purpose of insurance claims investigations, court proceedings, notice for towed or impounded vehicles, bulk marketing, motor vehicle market research, or (ironically, given the details of the Rebecca Schaeffer case) private investigators.[33] Those loopholes have proven to be a cash cow for states scraping for funds under neoliberal tax regimes. DMVs—including in Indiana and New York, where most of our interviewees live and drive—peddle their data for millions.[34] Both the geolocation data (from ALPR scans) and the DMV data are commodities that are sold to the same lending and repossession firms that sustain the subprime car loan as a profitable enterprise. The South Carolina DMV, for example, made more than $42 million selling its data between 2015 and 2018. That information was purchased by insurance and credit ratings companies like Southern Farm Bureau and Experian.[35] In 2017, the Florida Department of Highway Safety and Motor Vehicles earned a whopping $77 million from data sales to "more than 30 private companies, including marketing firms, bill collectors, insurance companies and data brokers"[36]

While the automobile's computing power has itself become a profitable source of data for the manufacturer and the dealer, the owner of the car does not own this data. Nor is there any way for them to access it.

As vehicles come loaded with GPS systems, onboard cameras, sensors, and networked systems into which smartphones are plugged, "car-tapping" has become a new means of data mining. The telematics in automobiles now generate data for everything from locational frequency (where the driver shops, eats, prays, works), musical tastes, financing terms, and payment histories to fueling patterns, mileage, braking, and accelerating behavior, as well as video and audio data from onboard cameras. Such data can be cross-indexed with information drawn from smartphones plugged into the car (IP addresses, cookies, etc.). Police can readily obtain this data through a court order, and litigants can seek it in civil cases—including divorce and custody suits—through subpoena. Manufacturers increasingly exploit this "behavioral" data as a profit source, selling it onward to insurers, credit agencies, and marketing companies. In fact, McKinsey has projected that carmakers could control data valued at $750 billion by the end of the decade![37] This potential windfall, and its ominous consequences, are a lucid example of what legal scholar Shoshana Zuboff terms "surveillance capitalism."

Jumaane's Loan

Surveillance systems help to locate, ensnare, and discipline subprime borrowers, converting their risk into profit. Our interviewees told us that, after returning home from prison, they received endless texts, robocalls, and mail offering them credit cards and loans of various kinds. We cannot know if this is because their data was sold by the DMV after they reinstated their license or by a private entity after they signed a contract for a phone or applied for a bank card. But it is likely that the value of this data derives specifically from their subprime credit status, which marks them out as targets for predatory lending. Meanwhile, ALPR is only one of several new technologies that facilitate the profitable practice of repossession. Increasingly dealerships load kill switches into cars that they have financed with subprime loans. This allows them to remotely disable a car, as soon as a driver has missed a payment.[38] Such technologies, like the ALPR scans, streamline the process of repossession, which is an integral part of what we could call the subprime loan system.

Consider the loan obtained by Jumaane. He was in his early sixties when he returned home to Gary, Indiana, after more than thirty years in state prison. A Black radical, he had studied extensively while in prison, and served as a jailhouse lawyer, advising various inmates who sought his expertise. For the first year after his release, he rode a bicycle to get around. Then friends came together and gifted him a 1998 Toyota sedan. He used this car to get to his warehouse job, and considered himself lucky that he did not have to sleep in it as he moved between friends' couches during a period of homelessness. Three years after being released, he had a stable apartment and job, and he had saved $5,000. Then a letter came from Capital One. "Congratulations, you have been pre-approved for between $4,000 and $40,000 credit towards a new vehicle!"

Jumaane suspected that it was a trick, but the transmission had given out on his Toyota, and he was desperate. The letter directed him to a specific dealership. It included a barcode that he scanned with his phone, and a private number for him to call. When he called the dealership, they already knew he had scanned the barcode and encouraged him to "Come on in right away!" Just to be sure he was on the hook, they followed up with a series of text messages. He drove his dying car, which was now stuck in first gear, all the way to the sales lot, along with the $3,000 he set aside from his savings for a down payment.

Jumaane told us that he had been in the market for a "regular medium-sized pickup truck," so he could do extra side jobs like landscaping, lawn care, and hauling debris. When he sat down at the desk in the showroom, the salesman said they didn't have one in stock. "But then the dealer was waving his hand to me, saying 'Come outside.' And it was a truck he had parked there with all the doors open, had the hood open, and had the tailgate open, and had me walking around, looking at it." It had no price or sticker or label anywhere on it, but he was quoted a price of $25,000. Then the salesman turned up the pressure. "'Here—here it is right now. Right now. It's yours right now. Right now. You can walk out of here, this is your truck right now,' you know? And I'm like, 'I don't know, I got to think about this one, you know?' But they led me to believe that my credit was good, and that they would honor the Capital One offer. So I said, well what do I have to lose? And I said okay." Jumaane handed over his $3,000 deposit and drove off the lot with a 2015 Dodge Ram truck.

But when he returned to complete the paperwork the next day, "that's when they told me that Capital One would not finance it. So now they had to look around for another financial institution." Before he knew it, they had offered him a four-year loan with an interest rate in the high twenties, well above the state usury cap of 21 percent. He would be making monthly payments of $656 on the car plus another $165 for insurance. Jumaane no longer wanted the truck. "I kept saying, 'Well just take it back.' They didn't—they did not want to take that truck back. They kept trying to talk me into keeping it. 'Don't worry about it, it's not going to cost you a thing.'" Now he knew he was trapped, and resigned himself. That night, he looked up the model on Carfax and discovered his new $25,000 truck had a Blue Book value of only $18,000. When we spoke with him, he was single-mindedly focused on raising his credit score so that he could refinance.

If Jumaane, who makes minimum wage at a warehouse, winds up missing a payment on this predatory loan, the dealership can call in the repo man. They'll get back their truck, and they'll keep his hard-earned deposit and whatever payments they have already collected. Then they can repackage and sell it to the next subprime borrower they pull in with their bogus offers of easy credit. Jumaane's credit score will take a hit, and he will be back on his bicycle in the Indiana winter.

The Credit Score

The credit score is one of the primary channels through which much of the data mined by surveillance systems is fed. Anyone in the US has a legal right to access their credit report annually, but they do not own it. The report, from which the score is calculated, is the proprietary asset of the credit-reporting agency. It is compiled from our economic and social activity, but it is the property of the likes of Experian, Equifax, and TransUnion, the top three agencies that make billions of dollars each year by selling it. Nor are the results always accurate. More than a quarter of people surveyed by the Federal Trade Commission in 2013 had an error in their report. The survey also found that such errors disproportionately impacted people with less education.[39]

Many Americans do not have enough of a data trail in the formal banking and credit systems to generate a full report, or else that trail has grown cold through a period of dormancy. They are given a low score as a result. Not surprisingly, incarceration is "strongly correlated" with having a limited credit history.[40] With those sixty-five million "thin file" consumers in mind, the credit score industry has developed "alternative, big-data tools that promise lenders a way to 'squeeze additional performance' out of their underwriting."[41] One outcome is the emergence of new credit reporting start-ups beyond the big three companies. And this is where the car comes back into the picture. Over time, the constituent components of the credit score have become increasingly elaborate. To establish a score, more and more behavioral data is drawn into complex algorithms that sort through masses of data, including the information collected from the car—its geolocation patterns, a driver's media preferences, social network data, and consumption patterns. As the CEO of Zest Financial put it in an interview with *The New York Times*, "we feel like all data is credit data. We just don't know how to use it yet."[42]

Traditionally, the credit score offered a means for protecting creditors by determining who was at risk for defaulting on a loan. With the advent in the 1980s of "risk-based pricing" in lending, a low credit score became a source of handsome profits. Lenders discovered that if they charged enough in fees, interest, and inflated sales prices, they could still profit from buyers who were unlikely to repay a loan. As sociologist Barbara Kiviat puts it, "the chance a customer defaults and the chance that a customer is profitable are two different things."[43]

We have already seen how the DMV sells data, including to marketing firms, and how ALPR and behavioral data extracted from cars are sold onward. This makes it easier for "thin file" or subprime borrowers like Jumaane and Jeff to wind up targeted by dealerships for predatory loans. According to legal scholars Mikella Hurley and Julius Adebayo, "major data brokers, some of whom are also engaged in credit reporting, have been criticized for selling so-called 'sucker lists' that identify individuals who are 'old, in financial distress, or otherwise vulnerable to certain types of marketing pitches.'" They cite a Senate Commerce Committee report from 2013 that names some of these lists, with titles like "Hard Times," "Burdened by Debt," and "X-tra Needy," that are carefully designed to identify the consumers most susceptible to taking on rapacious loans.[44]

Of course, any such loan puts the borrower at risk of falling into an ever-tightening debt trap. If someone like Jumaane defaults on their high-interest loan, their credit score will take another hit, and they will in turn be charged more for a next loan, all of which pushes them further into debt. But the credit score is an even more powerful form of surveillance, and it is one that extends over many sectors of our daily economic life. Over the years credit reporting has morphed into a tool of character assessment, deployed for a multitude of purposes, from employment background checks and apartment rental application approvals (even in government-owned housing) to determining utility rates (and deposit requirements), hospital service fees, insurance premiums, and cell phone contracts.[45]

Jeff went to prison at age seventeen. When he emerged eight years later, he had supposedly "paid his debt to society" through the time he spent trapped in a cage. But this penal debt left him without a credit history and burdened with a felony record. He spent the first year out begging rides from family and coworkers to and from work and parole meetings. Then an uncle gifted him a dilapidated car, which he spent several months endlessly repairing. But he needed a more reliable form of transportation, so he tried a reputable dealership without luck and instead found himself at a "second-chance superstore," signing on to what he knew was a predatory loan. He checks his credit score every day. Meanwhile, the police check his plate, pull him over, and take their share. Sometimes when he is cruising down the highway in Indianapolis, he can feel like he is free. Other times, when cops come out of their patrol car with pistols in their hand, or when he forks over a tidy sum for interest on an overpriced car he can barely afford, it feels like anything but.

Beware the future of transportation.

Conclusion

Racism is like a Cadillac, they bring out a new model every year.
—Malcolm X

In the fall of 2021, we drove from New York City to Albany's MVP Arena (formerly known as the Knickerbocker Arena, the Pepsi Arena, and then the Times Union Center) to attend an annual car show sponsored by Hudson Valley dealerships. Roaming around the arena's staging areas, we stopped at several booths to ask about their willingness to work with potential buyers who had some credit problems. Every dealer assured us that subprime borrowers could be happily accommodated by one of the many banks with whom they had relationships—including such well-known subprime specialists as CAC, Santander, and Capital One. At one booth, though, we met with a different response. "No one should do that," a woman told us. "They will wind up paying twice as much for their car." We quickly learned she was a rep for the manufacturer, not a dealer.

She advised us that it would be better to take determined and calculated steps to raise a credit score than to enter into a subprime loan agreement. "In six months you can move from subprime to prime. Trust me, it's worth the wait." She told us she had learned this the hard way herself, after she lost everything but her kids ("The only thing I cared about!") in a divorce. She had been forced by circumstances to enter into high-interest borrowing and to rebuild her credit, so she spoke from experience, and with compassion. Meanwhile, a local dealer stood to the side, urging us to take his card, visibly eager to do business there and then. The more the rep cautioned us, the more solicitous the dealer became.

It could have been a good cop–bad cop routine, not untypical of the sales pitches that are the bread and butter of the industry. But we concluded that we had witnessed a moment of genuine honesty, even empathy, on her part. Or perhaps it was a symptom of how the swelling auto debt burden was finally impacting the carmaker's brand and taking its toll on the well-oiled business of peddling automobiles. There is some evidence, after all, that the soaring financial and ecological cost of private transportation is yielding a newly altered landscape in which personal ownership of cars (especially in their long-enduring "steel and petroleum" format) is no longer at the center.

Serving a provincial, regional market, the Albany event did not feature very many "cars of the future" of the kind that traditionally create a buzz around car shows with a display of gee-whizzery or supercar gadgetry. But the future of cars is a fast-morphing concept, well on its way to putting the standard, internal combustion models firmly in the rearview mirror. Two months earlier, Munich hosted IAA Mobility, a landmark reinvention of the car show that had occurred annually since 1897 as the Internationale Automobil-Ausstellung, famous for launching a long succession of classic German automobiles. The revamped show featured electric scooters and e-bikes, electric buses and trams, and transportation pods alongside the latest driverless vehicles. The convention panels were thick with talk about decarbonization, smart infrastructure, digital innovations, sustainable supply chains and fuels, and on-message appeals to the "mobility revolution."[1]

At cutting-edge shows like the new IAA, personal cars are no longer promoted as the main event. They are only one component of Mobility as a Service (MaaS), a corporate vision of the near-future which encompasses a variety of on-demand modes of transport—bicycle, e-scooter and EV car sharing, self-driving vehicles, taxibots, motorized skateboards, autonomous shuttles, pop-up bus service, software trains, ride-hailing, microtransit, and AV bus platoons, among others.[2] Given the widening gap between sticker prices and household incomes, the soaring costs of ownership, insurance, maintenance, and parking make less and less sense for drivers of vehicles that might sit idle for 96 percent of the day. Paying for transport only when needed is now touted as an affordable and carbon-efficient alternative. The key to this mobility landscape is the ability to seamlessly connect the trip options required to avoid the congestion, inconvenience, and dangers of driving across metro regions.

In one tempting promotional scenario, an electric cargo bike or driverless shuttle arrives at your door, as ordered, to take you and your stuff to the central train or urban air terminal, while a self-driving EV car is waiting at the rail station or airhub in another town. Even though you have never driven it before, that vehicle already knows a great deal about you—how you like your seat adjusted, your favorite music, your preferred routes, and your current mood—and it will deliver you to a destination as you nap, complete a work project, or watch a movie en route. Every vehicle is coordinated for you through a personal phone app, which also offers multiple options, priced accordingly, for each leg of the journey.

The benefits of this blueprint for self-driving, vehicle-sharing, and low-carbon transport are obvious.[3] But this smooth, technocratic version of a user-centric, networked future glosses over the darker side of the "mobility revolution." The digitization of our personal mobility has turned the cell phone into a treasure trove of valuable data, easily accessed and mined for the purposes of corporate and government surveillance. The "connected car" of the auto industry has evolved along a similar pathway, spying on us by routinely transmitting information about our behavior and phone use to the carmaker, for potential sale to any buyer. With MaaS on the horizon, the ability to more perfectly integrate and synchronize the surveillance capacities of all devices—the phone, the car, and other vehicles—is increasingly within reach. It's alarming to know that government agencies and corporations could be able to track every movement, location, purchase, and communication along the way.

For those with a carceral record or any history of traffic violations, there is every reason to fear this new data-driven dragnet. But public trust in the privacy protections of new technologies has been eroding for some time. With enhanced connectivity, cyberspace has filled up with hyper-aggressive commercial targeting, personal data breaches, and varieties of harassment, extortion, and harm generated by the systematic collection and sharing of information about our everyday conduct and life choices. The trade-off that platform capitalism offers—free, or cheap, access in return for the right to monetize our personal data—is a highly asymmetrical arrangement, fraught with potential for abuse and exploitation. Extending this domain of data surveillance to the open road—the mythic landscape of American liberties—is an ominous prospect.

As part of their pitch to "disrupt" the auto business, promoters of MaaS promise to remedy many of the problems described in this book. Shared self-driving cars and other vehicles, they vow, will not only be much safer, but will also eliminate the unsavory business of traffic stops, subprime loans, and revenue policing, each with its own racist record of preying on poverty and skin color. We are assured that their radar sensors, embedded supercomputers, advanced autopilots, and brain-to-vehicle technology (B2V) will make them too smart to make stupid mistakes or illegal moves. However, growing evidence that racism and other social prejudices get baked into new technologies, including the controversial algorithms that preside over more and more decision-making, suggests that this sunlit confidence may be premature.[4] The facial-recognition software that is already a component of police surveillance cameras has generated criti-cism of racial bias in Black and brown neighborhoods where these devices are disproportionately installed. As Simone Brown has described in *Dark Matters: On the Surveillance of Blackness*, such biometric technologies and practices have a long history dating to the trans-Atlantic slave trade.[5]

The Big Tech house style of breathlessly promoting cool new gadgets also turns a blind eye to the massive challenges of re-regulating a trans-portation infrastructure no longer centered on the individualistic model of personal ownership and self-directed motion. The legal, economic, and social culture of road rules and conduct will have to be transformed if shared and interconnected vehicles are going to be running the show. Traditional concerns about the policing of public and passenger safety will make room for new fears about cybersecurity intrusions (where hacked cars are wielded as weapons, as featured in the blockbuster film *The Fate of the Furious*), out-of-control vehicles driven by "deep learning" AI, or the harms generated by the automated tracking and profiling of groups targeted for police scrutiny. Personal data protection laws of the kind pioneered by EU legislators will increasingly be at odds with black-box legislation, favored by the auto and insurance industries. The latter requires new cars to incorporate "event data recorders" that document all manner of driving details for post-crash dissection, but this information can be all too easily abused when the carmaker, and not the driver, owns the data and controls what is collected.[6]

How will the mobility revolution transform a capitalist marketplace long defined by the nexus of cozy relationships between manufacturers, dealers, lenders, and insurers? Multi-billion-dollar investments have been pouring into the tech development of a driverless future that has long been heralded but is stubbornly resistant to materializing. The expectation of returns on these massive investments runs high. MaaS is already a fully-fledged corporate vision, crawling with VC funded start-ups and unicorns, and so heavy financialization of this new mobility landscape is a given, conducive to extracting revenue from every kind of movement, at any time.[7] Without corresponding levels of public investment in public infrastructure, the tollbooth economy looks as if it will expand exponentially. Under these circumstances, new forms of redlining and economic exclusion are almost certain to emerge.

So, too, it is difficult to conceive how municipalities and other local governments will be willing, or even able, to give up the loss of government revenue from parking and traffic fines. The installation of red light and speed cameras for detecting and penalizing violators has proven to be a reliable booster of revenue collections, but the mass introduction of driverless cars that are more compliant with the traffic code would result in steep reductions. No doubt, officials will look for other ways to offset the losses, with new kinds of curb pricing and road access fees, resulting in further privatization of public space. As for the highly lucrative business of auto lending, the existing model—dealer-driven, point-of-sale, and consumer-focused—will likely shift toward commercial transactions, with more and more loans going to owners of shared vehicle fleets. Money-spinning loans and leases will still be originated, underwritten, and sold, but they will no longer revolve solely around personally owned assets.[8]

On the other side of the ledger, the *Blueprint for Autonomous Urbanism*, produced by the National Association of City Transportation Officials (NACTO), aims to commandeer the MaaS vision as a way to "reclaim the street" from automobiles, reinstalling "people at the center of urban life." In the words of Janette Sadik-Khan, NACTO chair and former commissioner of New York's Department of Transportation, "the autonomous revolution will be humanized" through street redesign, de-prioritization of private vehicles, and comprehensive consumer data protection laws.[9] The massive volume of urban space set aside for parking and private automobility will be repurposed. More generally, the hope of AV advocates is that driverless transport will be much more inclusive of populations whose access to transportation has long been constrained by income, age, social isolation, and disability. As many as twenty-five million Americans have disabilities that limit their travel, while youth and the elderly are promised much more mobility in a self-driving future. In addition, instead of journey data being abused, the upgraded technical ability to track drivers and vehicles through MaaS could be used to detect and prevent trafficking and other forms of modern slavery.[10]

We welcome all such efforts to propel the mobility revolution in the direction of improved access, public safety, and financial affordability.

At the same time, we feel it necessary to draw attention to the racially uneven playing field that is often glossed over by such liberal technocratic visions of the future. Racial capitalism has a long and resilient history; it will not wither away without a bitter fight. Indeed, let us recall one of Malcolm X's most enduring quotes: "Racism is like a Cadillac, they bring out a new model every year." He made this pithy observation before the rise of mass incarceration; before automobile use was conscripted as an efficient vehicle for delivering Black and brown people into the arms of the carceral system; before the civil right to access loans was promoted by the financial industry as a form of predatory inclusion; and before government agencies seized upon racialized poverty as a source of revenue that was backed up by the threat of detention.

Extracting mobility from the carceral web is not achievable by technological change alone; it is deeply entangled in the laws, policing practices, policies of population control, and financial predation that sustain the web. A comprehensive approach is required to establish the right to free movement, which has never been fully extended or exercised. Prison abolitionists often cite Angela Davis's declaration that their movement's goal is not simply to do away with prisons, but to create the kind of society "that does not need prisons."[11] In that same spirit, detention, surveillance, and financial entrapment should have no place in the future world of mobility. In response to the long, historical record of controlling the movements of BIPOC individuals through public space, "mobility justice" has become a rallying cry for activists seeking to decriminalize and decolonize the right to move freely and with dignity, without fear of harassment, deportation, or death.[12] In this book, we have added debt servitude to that list, because the commercial and legal financial liabilities generated by car ownership and use are a key constraint on the freedom of movement.

The holistic analysis presented in these pages is intended to lend support to that comprehensive approach. We understand that reform advocates are obliged to pick their battles either with state-issued LFOs or with creditor-generated commercial debt, but from the perspective of someone held by the twenty-first-century debtors' prison, the distinction between the two matters very little. So, too, we have argued throughout this book that, for the vast majority of Americans who have no optional alternative to owning and using cars, it is not easy to avoid or escape from the octopus of debt and surveillance that sits astride the automobile economy. The state's twentieth-century policies of auto-centric growth and development and its full-throated backing of a fossil-driven, internal combustion technology (barely changed since its nineteenth-century invention) has ensured that vehicles prized for their exuberant, hand-operated motion have also served as devices for capturing an unjust share of household income, personal data, and individual liberty.

What we learned while researching and writing this book has bolstered our commitment to key principles that are widely violated under the current system, but that should be central to any philosophy or program of mobility justice. We firmly believe that neither poverty nor race should be the basis of profit or of criminalization—judges, sheriffs, lenders, or dealers who perpetuate these injustices should be heavily fined and barred from their practices, jobs, and businesses. We also believe that true freedom of movement requires comprehensive, and enhanced, protection of all vehicle operators and passengers, in addition to pedestrians. Realizing these principles will require the dismantling of traffic safety and auto delivery systems that are built on predatory policing and lending. To achieve that goal, mobility justice will have to push far beyond the decarbonization reforms being adopted by the auto industry and elected officials in the name of efficiency economics. In addition, the task will require reparative policymaking for past harms and future thriving for populations who have long been social, as well as physical, casualties of auto-centric policymaking.

To that end, then, we embrace the following positions suggested by the mobility, debt, and carceral justice movements. We believe that the entire carceral system is riddled with inequalities and injustices but, for the purposes of this book, our advocacy list is limited to items that are auto-related.

The first involves fundamental reforms to orient policing away from armed traffic stops for searches and revenue collection and toward community safety and well-being. While we acknowledge that the roads traversed by enormous steel vehicles are potentially dangerous, and that public spaces need regulation and monitoring, the long record of harms and human rights violations calls out for armed police officers to be withdrawn from traffic duties, just as they are have been from parking and tollbooth enforcement. Furthermore, we advocate a move to income-graduated traffic fines for infractions that legitimately concern public safety, so that wealthy motorists face meaningful disincentives for unsafe conduct while low-income drivers no longer suffer disproportionately punitive outcomes for the same behaviors.

Such policies must be combined with strict usury caps on automobile loans and, ideally, with the setting of federal limits at significantly lower rates than the current norm in most states. All loopholes allowing lenders to conceal fees and real APRs, to set finance charges at the higher rates permitted in their home states, and to evade statutory limits by other means, need to be closed. Subprime lenders who issue credit in the full knowledge that borrowers cannot service their debts and will forfeit their vehicles as a result should be put out of business, not slapped on the wrist with fines. Wherever the market securitization of loans encourages such behavior, it should be prohibited.

There can be no justice without the swift and complete closure of the back door to debtor's prison, through which collection agencies and creditors enlist the courts in judgments that ignore inability to pay. In that regard, we insist that constitutionally minded decisions against excessive fines and unfair treatment like *Bearden v. Georgia* and *Timbs v. Indiana* be properly observed as the law of the land, in all courts. Cash bail, which disproportionately penalizes poor people, should be abolished along with the practice of issuing arrest warrants in debt collection cases. The widespread use of revenue policing, much of it directed at extracting traffic fines and fees, calls out for comprehensive reform. Municipal services should be funded by progressive taxation and not by preying on otherwise law-abiding motorists.

The all-too-common errors that plague the technologies of credit and surveillance are unacceptable. We call for the establishment of maximum error thresholds beyond which agencies and businesses should be heavily penalized for their improper use of faulty technologies. Why should consumers have to be subject to a nontransparent and chronically flawed credit-reporting system, or be surveilled by ALPR technologies that regularly misread at high rates? Why should we allow the state to impose late penalties for overdue fees and fines while neglecting to penalize government and corporate employees for such egregious bureaucratic and technological failures?

Looking forward, we recommend policies that curb the rapidly expanding surveillance regime outlined in the previous chapter. The US should adopt a robust version of the EU's General Data Protection Regulation to ensure a high level of privacy protections from Silicon Valley data capture and commodification. New law enforcement technologies like surveillance drones or military-grade X-ray (backscatter) vans, which can reveal the entire contents of private vehicles to police, should be prohibited as excessively intrusive or require warrants, and only for limited and socially beneficial uses. Police departments should be demilitarized, starting with the dismantling of technology transfer programs from the Department of Defense.

Finally, we see in mobility justice the potential for reparation of past harms. A redesign or retrofit of transportation infrastructure is needed to remediate the trauma and social damage generated by the development policies of the past seventy years. As Transportation Secretary Pete

Buttigieg publicly acknowledged, one place to start is by demolishing the urban freeways that were driven through the heart of low-income communities. Any such demolition must be accompanied by efforts to improve access to safe infrastructure—sidewalks, crosswalks, and bike lanes—that is chronically lacking in these communities. The US badly needs new investments in public transit of all kinds. These commitments should be aimed in particular at underserved communities while bundling affordable housing initiatives near new rail lines and transit hubs. We believe that public transportation including bike-sharing and micro-mobility options should be free and well-maintained. We are demanding a future where mass transit is as status-rich and pleasurable as the bullet train.

The formerly incarcerated persons whom we interviewed for this book helped us understand the tremendous discipline and drive it takes for most people emerging from prison to succeed in a reentry process that is rife with bureaucratic, financial, practical, and social challenges. One false move and it is easy to find yourself sleeping on the street or back in a cage. Each of our interviewees had at one time been confined for years, and most had lost everything they owned as a result of incarceration. Their experiences upon release of walking for miles to meetings with a parole office, or pedaling a decrepit ten-speed bike on the side of an icy road to get groceries, or setting off each day on a predawn two-hour bus journey to work, were reminders of their status as mobility outcasts, and also of the sheer tenacity it would take to rebuild their lives. We heard how crucial the support of family and local organizations could be in their success—and how that support might take the form of rides, cosigned loans, or even a gifted car. We also saw the tremendous pressure many felt to do right by those who had supported them, and the tightly scripted regime of self-discipline many adopted in order to succeed. They were often surprised at first that we wanted to talk about cars, but they also understood why.

When we met with Mychal Pagan, whose photographs you see in this book, he told us that during his time in Sing Sing he counted the steps he took each day from his cell to the dining hall, to the library, and around the exercise yard. Those steps marked the limits of the cage that held him. But he also often sought out the small window in one room from which he could glimpse the Hudson River below. He said that that flowing water, constantly in motion, was freedom itself.

Our interviewees vividly remembered each car they had owned and how that vehicle marked a time in the arc of their life—the used black Toyota their stepfather had gifted them on their graduation from high school, or the '64 Impala with the immaculate leather interior that had been their youthful calling card. They recalled the Ford that their mother had crashed, the BMW in which they had been arrested, and the Jeep that had been seized and sold by police. A few who had once sold drugs reminisced about tricked-out, spotless, head-turning cars whose allure helped to broker their business and whose beauty got them laid. Some told stories from rural childhoods about sitting on their father's lap and turning the wheel while he pushed the pedals. Others spoke of riding around town with friends, of driving to Costco with their spouse, of road trips to visit relatives, of Pinterest boards they created for their Mini Cooper. Every single person had at least one uneasy story about being pulled over by police. Over and over, they used the word *freedom*.

Only one of the people with whom we spoke owned a home, but almost everyone—save a few people in New York City—owned a car. For most, that car was their single largest asset, and yet almost no one owned it outright. They were rightfully wary of car dealerships and knew when they were being sold a predatory loan. They were well aware of the practice of revenue policing and of the power of the DMV to extract money from them. They drove to avoid arrest, and they took on new debt and paid bills to raise their credit scores. Sometimes these strategies failed.

A Federal Reserve survey in 2019 showed that 40 percent of Americans would have difficulty raising $400 to cover an unforeseen expense like an emergency car repair.[13] But this often-cited statistic does not show how many of these same people have been drained of any financial resilience through the profiteering practices, like revenue policing and high-interest loans, that are investigated in this book. Of course, there are no comparable studies of how many people end up behind bars due to their inability to pay traffic fines or make loan payments. Nor is it possible to quantify the upshot of using the threat of detention as a debt collection tactic.

Yet the evidence we have laid out in these pages suggests that these practices, among others, are part and parcel of a systematic shakedown that feeds off compulsory car ownership and use. The coercion involved, whether it is administered by police, judges, jailers, lenders, credit agencies, or data miners, is a key element of our rigged creditocracy. As long as these agents of intimidation can be relied on to apply threats or impose penalties, the heady promise of the open road will remain just that.

Notes

Introduction

1   Stanford Open Policing Project, https://openpolicing.stanford.edu/findings/.

2   "Incarceration and Reentry," U.S. Department of Health and Human Services, https://aspe.hhs.gov/topics/human-services/incarceration-reentry-0.

3   The Prison Education Program Research Lab is a collaboration between faculty and students in NYU's Prison Education Program, https://wp.nyu.edu/nyu_debt_project/.

4   Throughout this book we use pseudonyms and at times alter distinguishing details in order to protect the privacy of formerly incarcerated interlocutors. We have been careful to ensure that any change in details we introduced is trivial and not substantive (e.g., disguising a Ford-model car by substituting a similar class of Chevrolet).

5   While men continue to be incarcerated in much larger numbers than women or transpersons, rates of incarceration for women have undergone a massive seven-fold rise over the past four decades, and women drivers make up an increasing share of traffic stops. "Incarcerated Women and Girls," The Sentencing Project (November 24, 2020), https://www.sentencingproject.org/publications/incarcerated-women-and-girls/; "Policing Women: Race and Gender Disparities in Police Stops, Searches, and Use of Force," Prison Policy Initiative (May 14, 2019), https://www.prisonpolicy.org/blog/2019/05/14/policingwomen/. On the other end, women, and especially women of color, earn lower wages and have increased caregiving responsibilities (60 percent of incarcerated women have minor children), which impacts their credit and transportation needs.

6   Although it is not directly invoked in the US Constitution, the right to free movement figures in the Articles of Confederation (Article 4) and it is featured prominently, as Article 13, in the UN Declaration of Human Rights. In *United States v. Wheeler* (1920), the Supreme Court ruled that the right to travel is indirectly protected in the Privileges and Immunities Clause of Article IV, Section 2 of the Constitution.

7   White House, "The American Jobs Plan" (March 31, 2021), https://www.whitehouse.gov/briefing-room/statements-releases/2021/03/31/fact-sheet-the-american-jobs-plan/.

8   H.R.3684—Infrastructure Investment and Jobs Act, 117th Congress (2021–2022), https://www.congress.gov/bill/117th-congress/house-bill/3684/text.

9   Kea Wilson, "Infrastructure Deal 'Worst Ratio for Transit Funding Since Nixon,'" *Streetsblog USA* (July 30, 2021), https://usa.streetsblog.org/2021/07/30/infrastructure-deal-worst-ratio-for-transit-funding-since-nixon/.

10   April Ryan, "Buttigieg Says Racism Built into US Infrastructure Was a 'Conscious Choice'" *The Grio* (April 6, 2021), https://thegrio.com/2021/04/06/pete-buttigieg-racism-us-infrastructure/.

11   Interview with Deborah Archer, "A Brief History Of How Racism Shaped Interstate Highways," NPR (April 7, 2021) https://www.npr.org/transcripts/984784455.

12   Deborah Archer, "'White Men's Roads Through Black Men's Homes': Advancing Racial Equity Through Highway Reconstruction," *Vanderbilt Law Review* 73 (2020): 1259, https://cdn.vanderbilt.edu/vu-wp0/wp-content/uploads/sites/278/2020/10/19130728/White-Mens-Roads-Through-Black-Mens-Homes-Advancing-Racial-Equity-Through-Highway-Reconstruction.pdf.

13   Karl Raitz, ed., *The National Road* (Baltimore: Johns Hopkins University Press, 1996).

14   Ralph Nader, "The Highway Lobby" (1972), https://nader.org/2002/08/29/the-highway-lobby/.

15   George Kennan, *Around the Cragged Hill: A Personal and Political Philosophy* (New York: Norton, 1993), 161-162.

16   David Gartman, *Auto Opium: A Social History of Automobile Design* (London: Routledge, 1994).

17   Ryan Felton, "Many Americans Are Overpaying for Their Car Loans," *Consumer Reports* (October 21, 2021), https://www.consumerreports.org/car-financing/many-americans-overpay-for-car-loans-a8076436935/.

18   Duane Overholt, *Stop Auto Fraud: Automotive Deceptive Sales Tactics and Predatory Lending Practices*, http://www.stopautofraud.com/primer.htm.

19   Kriston McIntosh et al., "Examining the Black-White Wealth Gap," Brookings Institution, https://www.brookings.edu/blog/up-front/2020/02/27/examining-the-black-white-wealth-gap/.

20   In his book, *Black Market: The Slave's Value in National Culture after 1865* (Chapel Hill: University of Carolina Press, 2020), Aaron Carico describes the postbellum experience of African Americans with debt of every kind—as sharecroppers, consumers of credit at general stores, and as guarantors for servicing the public debt incurred during the War of Emancipation.

21   Hoover never actually used the phrase in public, but the Republican Party touted it in a 1928 campaign advertisement heralding the coming age of "Republican prosperity."

22   "Criminal Justice Facts," The Sentencing Project, https://www.sentencingproject.org/criminal-justice-facts/. Ruth Wilson Gilmore offers an influential account of

the growth of the prison industry in *Golden Gulag: Prisons, Surplus, Crisis and Opposition in Globalizing California* (Berkeley: University of California Press, 2007). Following Gilmore, others have confirmed that this economic development model falls far short of expectations on a number of counts. See Tom Meagher and Christie Thompson's summary in "So You Think a New Prison Will Save Your Town?" *The Marshall Project* (June 14, 2016), https://www.themarshallproject.org/2016/06/14/so-you-think-a-new-prison-will-save-your-town. Though most rural prisons have failed to generate promised economic growth for local communities, the employment they do offer depends on criminal courts maintaining a steady supply of convicted offenders.

23   "Findings," Stanford Open Policing Project, https://openpolicing.stanford.edu/findings/.

24   "Average New-Vehicle Transaction Prices Top $45,000 for First Time," Kelley Blue Book, https://mediaroom.kbb.com/2021-10-13-Average-New-Vehicle-Transaction-Prices-Top-45,000-for-First-Time,-According-to-Kelley-Blue-Book.

25   "Record Share of New-Car Shoppers Jumped Into a $1,000+ Monthly Payment in June," Edmunds (June 30, 2022), https://www.edmunds.com/industry/press/record-share-of-new-car-shoppers-jumped-into-a-1000-monthly-payment-in-june-according-to-edmunds.html.

26   "New-Vehicle Affordability Declines Again in May, Typical Monthly Payment Hits New Record of $712," CoxAutomotive (June 15, 2022), https://www.coxautoinc.com/market-insights/may-2022-vai/.

27   Drew DeSilver, "Today's Electric Vehicle Market," Pew Research Reports (June 7, 2021), https://www.pewresearch.org/fact-tank/2021/06/07/todays-electric-vehicle-market-slow-growth-in-u-s-faster-in-china-europe/.

28   Journalist Geoffrey Fowler arranged to have a Chevy hacked to find out how much personal data was being recorded and transmitted to GM, in "What Does Your Car Know About You?" *Washington Post* (December 17, 2019), https://www.washingtonpost.com/technology/2019/12/17/what-does-your-car-know-about-you-we-hacked-chevy-find-out/.

29   Sam Biddle, "Your Car Is Spying on You," *The Intercept* (May 3, 2021), https://theintercept.com/2021/05/03/CAR-SURVEILLANCE-BERLA-MSAB-CBP/.

Chapter One

1   Lester Brown, Christopher Flavin, and Colin Norman, *Running on Empty: The Future of the Motor Car in an Oil-Short World* (New York: Norton, 1979); John Jerome, *The Death of the Automobile: The Fatal Effect of the Golden Era, 1955–1970*

(New York: Norton, 1972); Emma Rothschild, *Paradise Lost: The Decline of the Auto-Industrial Age* (New York: Random House, 1973).

2   Tom Voelk, "Rise of S.U.V.s: Leaving Cars in Their Dust, With No Signs of Slowing," *The New York Times* (May 21, 2020), https://www.nytimes.com/2020/05/21/business/suv-sales-best-sellers.html; Keith Bradsher, *High and Mighty SUVs: The World's Most Dangerous Vehicles and How they Got That Way* (New York: PublicAffairs, 2002).

3   Tom Motavalli, "Every Automaker's EV Plans Through 2035 And Beyond," *Forbes* (October 4, 2021), https://www.forbes.com/wheels/news/automaker-ev-plans/.

4   Michael Sivak, "Has Motorization in the U.S. Peaked?" Sustainable Worldwide Transportation, University of Michigan (January 2018), http://websites.umich.edu/~umtriswt/PDF/SWT-2018-2.pdf.

5   US Department of Transportation, *Transportation Statistics Annual Report* (Washington, DC: 2020), https://ntlrepository.blob.core.windows.net/lib/79000/79200/79277/TSAR_2020_Compressed_20210104.pdf.

6   Peter Norton, *Fighting Traffic: The Dawn of the Motor Age in the American City* (Cambridge, MA: MIT Press; 2011); Clay McShane, *Down the Asphalt Path: The Automobile and the American City* (New York: Columbia University Press, 1994), 176–86; Dan Albert, *Are We There Yet?: The American Automobile Past, Present, and Driverless* (New York: Norton, 2019).

7   Robert and Helen Lynd, *Middletown: A Study in American Culture* (New York: Harcourt Brace Jovanovich, 1929), 255–56.

8   Ibid, 256.

9   See Joseph Interrante, "The Road to Autopia: The Automobile and the Spatial Transformation of American Culture," in David Lanier Lewis and Laurence Goldstein, eds., *The Automobile and American Culture* (Ann Arbor: University of Michigan Press, 1983).

10   On the topic of consumer driving, see Wolfgang Sachs, *For Love of the Automobile: Looking Back into the History of our Desires*, trans. Don Reneau (Berkeley: University of California Press, 1984).

11   Roy D. Chapin, "The Motor's Part in Transportation," *Annals of the American Academy of Political and Social Science* (November 1, 1924), https://journals.sagepub.com/doi/10.1177/000271622411600101.

12   There is no shortage of evidence about the monopolistic intent of the coalition to replace mass transit, but theories about this campaign—"GM kicked the streetcar" in shorthand—are often designated as a "conspiracy" because the streetcar companies were in economic trouble before National City Lines, the acquisition

vehicle, snapped them up. Bradford Snell's legal argument at the heart of the charges against General Motors and others was presented to the US Senate's Committee of the Judiciary's Subcommittee on Antitrust and Monopoly in February 1974: *American Ground Transport: A Proposal for Restructuring the Automobile, Truck, Bus, and Rail Industries* (Washington, DC: U.S. Government Print Office, 1974). Also see Glenn Yago, *The Decline of Transit: Urban Transportation in German and U.S. Cities, 1900–1970* (New York: Cambridge University Press, 1984); and Sy Adler, "The Transformation of the Pacific Electric Railway: Bradford Snell, Roger Rabbit, and the Politics of Transportation in Los Angeles," Vol. 27, *Urban Affairs Quarterly* (1991).

13   Virginia Scharff, *Taking the Wheel: Women and the Coming of the Motor Age* (New York: Free Press, 1991).

14   See Jane Pollard, Evelyn Blumenberg, and Stephen Brumbaugh, "Driven to Debt: Social Reproduction and (Auto)Mobility in Los Angeles," *Annals of the American Association of Geographers* Vol. 3, no. 5 (2021): 1445–1461.

15   Philip Deloria discusses white American outrage at the spectacle of American Indians, in traditional clothing, driving technologically advanced cars, in *Indians in Unexpected Places* (Lawrence: University Press of Kansas, 2004).

16   Sally Hadden, *Slave Patrols: Law and Violence in Virginia and the Carolinas* (Cambridge: Harvard University Press, 2001); Tony Platt, *The Iron Fist and the Velvet Glove: An Analysis of the U.S. Police* (San Francisco: Crime and Social Justice Associates, 1982).

17   See Danielle McGuire, *At the Dark End of the Street: Black Women, Rape, and Resistance: A New History of the Civil Rights Movement from Rosa Parks to the Rise of Black Power* (New York: Vintage, 2011).

18   Robert Caro, *The Power Broker: Robert Moses and the Fall of New York* (New York: Vintage, 1975), 318.

19   William Loewen, *Sundown Towns: A Hidden Dimension of American Racism* (New York: New Press, 2005).

20   Gretchen Sorin, *Driving While Black: African American Travel and the Road to Civil Rights* (New York: Norton, 2020), 18–33.

21   Dayson Brooks, *The Talk: Discussing Black America* (New York: Atlantic Publishing, 2020). Bobby Kimbrough presents popular advice, from a security and law enforcement perspective, in *Surviving The Stop: Change The Atmosphere, Change The Outcome* (New York: Perfect Publishers, 2016).

22   Sorin, *Driving While Black,* 50–66.

23   An often-cited example of white indignation at Black drivers was the public fury directed at Jack Johnson, the world heavyweight boxing champion who drove

ostentatiously, often with white women in the passenger seat, and whose 1910 match race with Barney Oldfield, a white racing driver, was widely regarded as a threat to racial and gender supremacy.

24   Sorin, *Driving While Black*, 70.

25   Genevieve Carpio, *Collisions at the Crossroads: How Place and Mobility Make Race* (Berkeley: University of California Press, 2019), 47–63, 75–88.

26   Carpio, *Collisions*, 144.

27   Carpio, *Collisions*, 1–5, 224–30.

28   A class action suit filed in 2007 found the Maricopa County Sheriff's Office guilty of racial profiling and unlawful traffic stops of Latinx drivers. See its "Findings of Fact and Conclusion of Law" at https://www.mcso.org/home/showpublisheddocument/658/637237842705100000.

29   Ray Stern, "Sheriff Joe Arpaio's Office Commits Worst Racial Profiling in U.S. History, Concludes DOJ Investigation," *Phoenix New Times* (December 15, 2011), https://www.phoenixnewtimes.com/news/sheriff-joe-arpaios-office-commits-worst-racial-profiling-in-us-history-concludes-doj-investigation-6655328. The Department of Justice investigation was launched in 2009: https://www.justice.gov/sites/default/files/crt/legacy/2011/12/15/mcso_findletter_12-15-11.pdf. The DOJ lawsuit was filed in 2012: https://www.justice.gov/sites/default/files/crt/legacy/2012/07/18/mcso_complaint_5-10-12.pdf.

30   See the 2012 DOJ investigation report of the Alamance County Sheriff's Office in North Carolina, at https://www.justice.gov/iso/opa/resources/171201291812462488198.pdf, and the 2011 DOJ investigation report of East Haven Police Department in Connecticut, at https://www.justice.gov/sites/default/files/crt/legacy/2011/12/19/easthaven_findletter_12-19-11.pdf.

31   Terry Greene Sterling and Jude Joffe-Block, *Driving While Brown: Sheriff Arpaio Versus The Latino Resistance* (Berkeley: University of California Press, 2021).

32   Ben Chappell, *Lowrider Space: Aesthetics and Politics of Mexican American Custom Cars* (Austin: University of Texas Press, 2012). Amy Best surveys the landscape of youth and car obsession in *Fast Cars, Cool Rides: The Accelerating World of Youth and Their Cars* (New York: NYU Press, 2006).

33   Paul Gilroy, "Driving While Black," in Daniel Miller, ed., *Car Cultures* (Oxford and New York: Berg, 2001), 81–104.

34   Michelle Alexander presents the broader analysis that mass incarceration is only the latest form of racialized social control in *The New Jim Crow: Mass Incarceration in the Age of Colorblindness, tenth anniversary edition* (New York: New Press, 2020). Also see Elizabeth Hinton, *From the War on Poverty to the War on Crime: The Making of Mass Incarceration* (Cambridge: Harvard University Press, 2016).

35   lgernon Austin, et al., *Stick Shift: Autonomous Vehicles, Driving Jobs, and the Future of Work*, Center for Global Policy Solutions (March 2017), http://globalpolicysolutions.org/wp-content/uploads/2017/03/cgps-autonomous-cars.pdf.

36   The continuity between labor on the inside and outside is explored in Erin Hatton, ed., *Labor and Punishment: Work in and out of Prison* (Berkeley: University of California Press, 2021).

37   Honda was heavily criticized for sourcing some of its car parts production to Ohio prisons. Gordon Lafer, "Captive Labor," *The American Prospect* (December 15, 2001), https://prospect.org/labor/captive-labor/. See the Marshall Project's dossier of reporting on prison labor, at https://www.themarshallproject.org/records/764-prison-labor. The ACLU's 2022 report, *Captive Labor: Exploitation of Incarcerated Workers*, surveys the state of prison labor nationwide. https://www.aclu.org/report/captive-labor-exploitation-incarcerated-workers.

38   Vehicular Upfit/De-Retro Services, UNICOR, https://www.unicor.gov/Product.aspx?idProduct=3862.

39   See Charles Epp, Steven Maynard-Moody, and Donald Haider-Markel, *Pulled Over: How Police Stops Define Race and Citizenship* (Chicago: University of Chicago Press, 2014); and R. Baumgartner, Derek Epp, and Kelsey Shoub, *Suspect Citizens: What 20 Million Traffic Stops Tell Us About Policing and Race* (Cambridge: Cambridge University Press, 2018).

40   The legacy of that class war continues. In her book *Right of Way: Race, Class, and the Silent Epidemic of Pedestrian Deaths in America (*Washington, DC: Island Press, 2020), Angie Schmitt shows that immigrants and poor pedestrians are overwhelmingly victims of traffic fatalities.

41   Sarah A. Seo, *Policing the Open Road: How Cars Transformed American Freedom* (Cambridge: Harvard University Press, 2019), 4.

42   Seo, *Policing*, 19.

43   For testimony that supports the procedural paradigm of a case-by-case consideration, see Nick Selby et al., *In Context: Understanding Police Killing of Unarmed Civilians* (CIAI Press, 2016).

44   Seo, *Policing*, 264-66.

45   For trenchant analyses of the need to radically diminish policing powers, see Alex Vitale, *The End of Policing* (New York: Verso, 2018); Geo Maher, *A World Without Police: How Strong Communities Make Cops Obsolete* (New York: Verso, 2021); and Kristian Williams, *Our Enemies in Blue: Police and Power in America* (AK Press, 2015).

46   Mapping Police Violence, data consulted up to April 7, 2022, https://mappingpoliceviolence.us/.

47 "Pedestrian Fatalities in New York City," New York City Department of Health and Mental Hygiene (March 2017), https://www1.nyc.gov/assets/doh/downloads/pdf/epi/databrief86.pdf.

48 Radley Balko, *Rise of the Warrior Cop: The Militarization of America's Police Forces* (New York: PublicAffairs, 2014). Technically, what is widely known as the 1033 program is amendment 2576a to Chapter 153 of Title 10 of the US Code, which gives the secretary of defense permanent authority to transfer excess defense matériel to law enforcement agencies. The latest version (post 2018) can be found at https://www.law.cornell.edu/uscode/text/10/2576a.

49 The impression is less striking when considered against the historical backdrop of the links between domestic policing and American contributions to imperial policing in overseas hot spots. See Stuart Schrader, *Badges without Borders: How Global Counterinsurgency Transformed American Policing* (Berkeley: University of California Press, 2019).

50 Barry Friedman makes links between discriminatory traffic stops and state surveillance of citizens in *Unwarranted: Policing Without Permission* (New York: Farrar, Straus and Giroux, 1974).

Chapter Two

1 Tommaso Bardelli, Ruqaiyah Zarook, and Derick McCarthy, "How Corporations Turned Prison Tablets Into a Predatory Scheme," *Dissent* (March 7, 2022), https://www.dissentmagazine.org/online_articles/corporations-prison-tablets-predatory-scheme.

2 Bruce Western, *Homeward: Life in the Year after Prison* (New York: Russell Sage Foundation, 2018); David J. Harding, Jeffrey D. Morenoff, and Jessica J. B. Wyse, *On the Outside: Prisoner Reentry and Reintegration* (Chicago: University of Chicago Press, 2019).

3 See Keeanga Yamahtta-Taylor, *Race for Profit: How Banks and the Real Estate Industry Undermined Black Homeownership* (Chapel Hill: University of North Carolina Press, 2019).

Chapter Three

1 Brett Simpson, "The Other Speed Trap," *The Atlantic* (February 2, 2022), https://www.theatlantic.com/ideas/archive/2022/02/traffic-tickets-income-adjustment-rich/621452/.

2   In *The New Debtors' Prison: Why All Americans Are in Danger of Losing Their Freedom* (New York: Skyhorse, 2019), 108, Christopher Maselli claims that more than 20 percent of the prison population is incarcerated for financial reasons such as failing to pay a fine, but we were unable to verify this statistic.

3   David Kirkpatrick et al., "Why Many Police Traffic Stops Turn Deadly," *The New York Times* (October 31, 2021), https://www.nytimes.com/2021/10/31/us/police-traffic-stops-killings.html.

4   Tanvi Misra, "Another Consequence of Traffic Stops: Deportation," *Bloomberg CityLab* (June 9, 2021), https://www.bloomberg.com/news/articles/2021-06-09/another-consequence-of-traffic-stops-deportation.

5   The 2003 to 2020 data on Immigration and Customs Enforcement Removals can be found at https://trac.syr.edu/phptools/immigration/remove/.

6   See Beth A. Colgan, "Excessive Fines Clause: Challenging the Modern Debtors' Prison," *UCLA Law Review* 65 (2018): 47–76.

7   See, for example, the work of the Fines and Fees Justice Center, https://finesandfeesjusticecenter.org/.

8   Mike McIntire and Michael H. Keller, "The Demand for Money Behind Many Police Traffic Stops," *The New York Times* (October 31, 2021), https://www.nytimes.com/2021/10/31/us/police-ticket-quotas-money-funding.html.

9   *Bearden v. Georgia* (1983), at https://supreme.justia.com/cases/federal/us/461/660/.

10   See these two reports from Human Rights Watch: *Profiting from Probation: America's "Offender-Funded" Probation Industry* (February 4, 2014), https://www.hrw.org/report/2014/02/05/profiting-probation/americas-offender-funded-probation-industry#; and *Set Up to Fail: The Impact of Offender-Funded Private Probation* (February 2021), https://www.hrw.org/report/2018/02/21/set-fail/impact-offender-funded-private-probation-poor#:~:text=The%20cost%20of%20private%20probation,in%20a%20report%20released%20today.

11   Chris Albin-Lackey, *Profiting from Probation: America's "Offender-Funded" Probation Industry*, Human Rights Watch (February 5, 2014), https://www.hrw.org/report/2014/02/05/profiting-probation/americas-offender-funded-probation-industry.

12   Alexes Harris, *A Pound of Flesh: Monetary Sanctions as Punishment for the Poor* (New York: Russell Sage Foundation 2016). In part as a result of her research, the Seattle Municipal Court judges voted to eliminate all discretionary fines and fees in criminal cases in September 2020.

13   Karin D. Martin, Sandra Susan Smith, and Wendy Still, *Shackled to Debt: Criminal Justice Financial Obligations and the Barrier to Re-entry They Create* (U.S. Department of Justice, Office of Justice Programs, National Institute of Justice,

2017); Alicia Bannon, Mitali Nagrecha, and Rebekah Diller, *Criminal Justice Debt: A Barrier to Reentry* (New York: Brennan Center for Justice at New York University School of Law, 2010), https://www.brennancenter.org/publication/criminaljustice-debt-barrier-reentry.

14   Ella Baker Center for Human Rights, Forward Together, Research Action Design et al., *Who Pays? The True Cost of Incarceration on Families* (September 2015), http://whopaysreport.org/who-pays-full-report/.

15   William E. Crozier and Brandon L. Garrett, "Driven to Failure: An Empirical Analysis of Driver's License Suspension in North Carolina," *Duke Law Journal* 69 (2020): 1588.

16   Fines and Fees Justice Center, *Free to Drive: National Campaign to End Debt-Based License Restrictions*, https://finesandfeesjusticecenter.org/campaigns/national-drivers-license-suspension campaign-free-to-drive/.

17   Matthew Menendez, Michael F. Crowley, Lauren-Brooke Eisen, and Noah Atchison, *The Steep Costs of Criminal Justice Fees and Fines: A Fiscal Analysis of Three States and Ten Counties* (New York: Brennan Center for Justice at NYU Law School, 2019), https://www.brennancenter.org/our-work/research-reports/steep-costs-criminal-justice-fees-and-fines; Emily Dindial, Emily Greytak, and Kana Tateishi, *Reckless Lawmaking: How Debt-Based Driver's License Suspension Laws Impose Harm and Waste Resources*, American Civil Liberties Union (2021), https://www.aclu.org/sites/default/files/field_document/reckless_lawmaking_aclu_final_4.19.21.pdf.

18   Driven by Justice, *Opportunity Suspended: How New York's Traffic Debt Suspension Laws Disproportionately Harm Low-Income Communities and Communities of Color*, https://www.drivenbyjustice.org/.

19   Back on the Road California, *Stopped, Fined, Arrested: Racial Bias in Policing and Traffic Courts in California* (April 2016), http://ebclc.org/wp-content/uploads/2016/04/Stopped_Fined_Arrested_BOTRCA.pdf.

20   Cited in Danielle Conley and Ariel Levinson-Waldman, "Discriminatory Driver's License Suspension Schemes," American Constitution Society (March 19, 2019), https://www.acslaw.org/issue_brief/briefs-landing/discriminatory-drivers-license-suspension-schemes/#_ednref42.

21   United States Department of Justice Civil Rights Division, *The Ferguson Report: Department of Justice investigation of the Ferguson Police Department* (2015), 16, https://www.justice.gov/sites/default/files/opa/press-releases/attachments/2015/03/04/ferguson_police_department_report.pdf.

22   Ibid., 5.

23   Angela LaScala-Gruenewald, Katie Adamides, and Melissa Toback, *New York's Ferguson Problem,* Fines and Fees Justice Center/No Price on Justice Coalition (February 2020), https://nopriceonjustice.org/wp-content/uploads/2020/09/New_York_Ferguson_Problem_NPJ_Report.pdf; Lawyers' Committee for Civil Rights of the San Francisco Bay Area et al., *Not Just a Ferguson Problem – How Traffic Courts Drive Inequality in California* (2015), https://lccrsf.org/wp-content/uploads/2021/05/Not-Just-a-Ferguson-Problem-How-Traffic-Courts-Drive-Inequality-in-California-2015.pdf.

24   Mike Maciag, "Local Government Fine Revenues by State," *Governing* (September 2019), https://www.governing.com/archive/local-governments-high-fine-revenues-by-state.html.

25   Dick Carpenter, Kyle Sweetland, and Jennifer McDonald, "The Price of Taxation by Citation," Institute for Justice (October 24, 2019), https://ij.org/wp-content/uploads/2019/10/Taxation-by-Citation-FINAL-USE.pdf. A 2021 investigation of three states—Ohio, Oklahoma, and Virginia—found the practice of ordering traffic citation quotas to be rife in many small city or town jurisdictions. Mike McIntire and Michael H. Keller, "The Demand for Money Behind Many Police Traffic Stops," *The New York Times* (October 31, 2021), https://www.nytimes.com/2021/10/31/us/police-ticket-quotas-money-funding.html.

26   Robert J. Thompson, "Unreasonable Traffic Fines Violate Constitutional Rights," *Fresno Bee* (August 24, 2015), https://www.fresnobee.com/opinion/op-ed/article32237655.html.

27   *In for a Penny: The Rise of America's New Debtors' Prisons,* ACLU (October 2010), 9, https://www.aclu.org/sites/default/files/field_document/InForAPenny_web.pdf.

28   Menendez, Crowley, Eisen, and Atchison, *The Steep Costs of Criminal Justice Fees and Fines: A Fiscal Analysis of Three States and Ten Counties.*

29   Vanita Gupta and Lisa Foster, "Letter Regarding Law Enforcement Fines and Fees," U.S. Department of Justice, Civil Rights Division Office for Access to Justice (March 14, 2016), https://www.courts.wa.gov/subsite/mjc/docs/DOJDearColleague.pdf; Matt Apuzzo, "Justice Dept. Condemns Profit-Minded Court Policies Targeting the Poor," *The New York Times* (March 14, 2016), https://www.nytimes.com/2016/03/15/us/politics/justice-dept-condemns-profit-minded-court-policies-targeting-the-poor.html.

30   On the implicit collusion of judges and lawyers, see Alec Karakatsanis, *Usual Cruelty: The Complicity of Lawyers in the Criminal Injustice System* (New York: New Press, 2019).

31   Heather Giles, "Covid-19 Pandemic Drives Municipal Borrowing to 10-Year High," *Wall Street Journal* (January 12, 2021), https://www.wsj.com/articles/covid-19-pandemic-drives-municipal-borrowing-to-10-year-high-11610447402.

32   See Destin Jenkins, *The Bonds of Inequality: Debt and the Making of the American City* (Chicago: University of Chicago Press, 2021).

33   Figures are from Debt Portfolio Information, MTA (July 16, 2021), https://new.mta.info/investor-info/debt-portfolio-information, and the estimate is from the Financial Outlook for the Metropolitan Transportation Authority (April 2021) of the NY State Comptroller, Thomas P. DiNapoli, https://www.osc.state.ny.us/files/reports/osdc/pdf/report-5-2021.pdf.

34   The Urban Institute, "Criminal Justice Expenditures: Police, Corrections, and Courts," https://www.urban.org/policy-centers/cross-center-initiatives/state-and-local-finance-initiative/state-and-local-backgrounders/criminal-justice-police-corrections-courts-expenditures.

35   Zusha Elinson, Dan Frosch, and Joshua Jameson, "Cities Reverse Defunding the Police Amid Rising Crime,"*Wall Street Journal* (May 26, 2021), https://www.wsj.com/articles/cities-reverse-defunding-the-police-amid-rising-crime-11622066307.

36   See Michael Hudson, *Killing the Host: How Financial Parasites and Debt Bondage Destroy the Global Economy* (New York: ISLET, 2015).

37   Michael Lind, "The Politics of Tollbooth Capitalism," *American Affairs* Vol. 5, Issue 1 (Spring 2021), https://americanaffairsjournal.org/issue/spring-2021/.

38   Mike Maciag, "Addicted to Fines: A Special Report," *Governing* (August 19, 2019), https://www.governing.com/archive/fine-fee-revenues-special-report.html.

39   U.S. Commission on Civil Rights, "Targeted Fines and Fees Against Communities of Color: Civil Rights & Constitutional Implications" (September 2017), https://www.usccr.gov/pubs/2017/Statutory_Enforcement_Report2017.pdf.

40   The Fund for Modern Courts, *Fines and Fees and Jail Time in New York Town and Village Justice Courts: The Unseen Violation of Constitutional and State Law* (April 3, 2019), http://moderncourts.org/wp-content/uploads/2019/04/Fines-and-Fees-and-Jail-Time-in-New-York-Town-and-Village-Justice-Courts-The-Unseen-Violation-of-Constitutional-and-State-Law.pdf. According to the State Comptroller, "[In 2009] about 90 percent of [the town and village court] revenue was generated through fines, fees and surcharges on vehicle and traffic violations, and smaller amounts were generated from forfeited bail and violations of environmental, penal and other laws." Office of the State Comptroller, *Report on the Justice Court Fund* (2010), https://www.osc.state.ny.us/files/local-government/publications/pdf/justicecourtreport2010.pdf.

41   New York City Bar Association, "New York Should Re-Examine Mandatory
      Court Fees" (May 9, 2019), https://www.nycbar.org/member-and-career-services/
      committees/reports-listing/reports/detail/new-york-should-re-examine-
      mandatory-court-fees#_ftn33.

42   "The fact that certain revenues are earmarked to fund these programs does not mean
      the revenues are used only for those purposes. Under certain circumstances, the State
      may elect to 'sweep' revenue from these funds into the General Fund." Office of the
      State Comptroller, *Report on the Justice Court Fund*, footnote 33. Among the monies
      swept from such funds in 2020, according to the state's FY 2021 Enacted Budget
      Financial Plan, $22 million was taken from the Criminal Justice Improvement Account,
      $17 million from the Legal Services Assistance Fund, $66 million from the Dedicated
      Highway and Bridge Trust Fund, and $1.12 *billion* from the State Police Motor Vehicle
      Enforcement Account. https://www.budget.ny.gov/pubs/archive/fy21/enac/fy21-
      enacted-fp.pdf (See T-212-13).

43   Glenn Blain, "Cuomo Wants Fewer Plea Bargains and Higher Fees for Speeding
      Tickets," *New York Daily News* (January 24, 2013), https://www.nydailynews.com/
      new-york/cuomo-crackdown-speeders-article-1.1247298.

44   "Best Practices Guide to Reducing Suspended Drivers," American Association of
      Motor Administrators (2013), https://www.aamva.org/Suspended-and-Revoked-
      Drivers-Working-Group/.

45   Editorial, "Train the Police to Keep the Peace, Not Turn a Profit," *The New York
      Times* (November 20, 2021), https://www.nytimes.com/2021/11/20/opinion/police-
      traffic-stops-deaths.html.

46   See Jordan Blair Woods, "Traffic Without the Police," *Stanford Law Review*, Vol. 73,
      1471 (2021).

47   Randy Petersen, "Let's Consider Traffic Enforcement," *Right on Crime* (January 17,
      2019), https://rightoncrime.com/2019/01/lets-reconsider-traffic-enforcement/.

48   Ella Baker Center for Human Rights, *Who Pays? The True Cost of Incarceration on
      Families.*

49   Alabama Appleseed Center for Law and Justice, *Under Pressure: How Fines and Fees
      Hurt People, Undermine Public Safety, and Drive Alabama's Racial Wealth Divide*
      (October 2018), https://www.alabamaappleseed.org/wp-content/uploads/2018/10/
      AA1240-FinesandFees-10-10-FINAL.pdf.

50   James Baldwin, "Fifth Avenue, Uptown," *Esquire* (July 1960).

51   "Preliminary Semiannual Estimates," National Safety Council (2021), https://
      injuryfacts.nsc.org/motor-vehicle/overview/preliminary-estimates/.

52   Ralph Nader, *Unsafe at Any Speed: The Designed-In Dangers of the American Automobile* (New York: Grossmann, 1972); Jerry Mashaw and David Harfst, *The Struggle for Auto Safety* (Cambridge: Harvard University Press, 1990).

53   For example, a study by Dara Lee Luca showed that a 1 percent increase in tickets issued in Massachusetts led to a 0.2 percent decline in motor vehicle crashes. "Do Traffic Tickets Reduce Motor Vehicle Accidents? Evidence from a Natural Experiment," *Journal of Policy Analysis and Management* 34, no. 1 (2015): 85–106.

54   Kea Wilson, "Do Traffic Fines Make Streets Safer—And at What Cost?" *Streetsblog USA* (April 29, 2021), https://usa.streetsblog.org/2021/04/29/do-automated-cameras-make-our-streets-safer/.

55   Transportation Alternatives, "The Case for Self-Enforcing Streets" (June 18, 2020), https://static1.squarespace.com/static/5cab9d9b65a707a9b36f4b6c/t/5eec1235fe73d720da412589/1592529462229/CaseForSelfEnforcingStreets.pdf.

56   Emma Whitford, "Report: The NYPD Is Failing Vision Zero," *Gothamist* (July 28, 2016), https://gothamist.com/news/report-the-nypd-is-failing-vision-zero.

57   Winnie Hu, "De Blasio Vowed to Make City Streets Safer: They Have Turned More Deadly," *The New York Times* (September 30, 2021), https://www.nytimes.com/2021/09/30/nyregion/traffic-deaths-nyc.html.

58   Alexandra Natapoff, *Punishment Without Crime: How Our Massive Misdemeanor System Traps the Innocent and Makes America More Unequal* (New York: Basic Books, 2018), 41.

59   See Wendy Sawyer and Peter Wagner, "Mass Incarceration: The Whole Pie," Prison Policy Initiative (March 24, 2020), https://www.prisonpolicy.org/reports/pie2020.html. Their estimate is based on figures from 2016 and 2017 Bureau of Justice Statistics data.

60   See Jackie Wang's chapter on "Policing as Plunder" in *Carceral Capitalism* (New York: Semiotexte, 2019).

61   Issa Kohler-Hausmann, *Misdemeanorland: Criminal Courts and Social Control in an Age of Broken Windows Policing* (Princeton: Princeton University Press, 2018).

62   Abby Shafroth and Larry Schwartzol, *Confronting Criminal Justice Debt: A Comprehensive Project for Reform* (Criminal Justice Policy Program of Harvard Law School and the National Consumer, September 2016).

63   Debt Free Justice California, "Governor Signs Historic Bill Repealing Unjust Criminal Justice Fees in California" (September 21, 2020), https://www.law.berkeley.edu/wp-content/uploads/2020/09/California-Governor-Signs-Historic-Bill-Abolishing-Unjust-Criminal-Fees-9-21-20-1-1.pdf.

64   "Policing Women: Race and Gender Disparities in Police Stops, Searches, and Use of Force," Prison Policy Initiative (May 14, 2019), https://www.prisonpolicy.org/blog/2019/05/14/policingwomen/.

Chapter Four

1   "Why America's Auto Debt Boom Fuels Bubble Talk," *Bloomberg* (March 23, 2017), https://www.bloomberg.com/news/articles/2017-03-23/why-america-s-auto-debt-boom-fuels-bubble-talk-quicktake-q-a; Jessica Silver-Greenberg and Michael Corkery, "In a Subprime Bubble for Used Cars, Borrowers Pay Sky-High Rates," *The New York Times* (July 19, 2014), https://dealbook.nytimes.com/2014/07/19/in-a-subprime-bubble-for-used-cars-unfit-borrowers-pay-sky-high-rates; Billy Nauman, "Why America's $1.3tn Car-Loan Market Cannot Avoid a Pile-Up," *Financial Times* (April 3, 2020), https://www.ft.com/content/5a8ca5b1-9a1c-4f81-99a5-acecef75b389; Chris Sorensen, "Is There an Auto Bubble on the Horizon?" *Macleans* (March 17, 2016), https://www.macleans.ca/economy/business/is-there-an-auto-bubble-on-the-horizon/.

2   Ben Winck, "People Have Stopped Paying Their Car Loans, and it Shows Millions are Struggling in this Economy," *Business Insider* (April 5, 20210, https://www.businessinsider.com/economic-recovery-subprime-borrowers-car-loans-delinquent-uneven-debt-coronavirus-2021-4.

3   David Lyons, "Repo Men Face a Big Year in 2021 as Car Payments go Overdue," *Fort Lauderdale Sun-Sentinel* (December 21, 2020), https://www.sun-sentinel.com/coronavirus/fl-ne-coronavirus-repo-men-eye-big-year-ss-prem-20201221-4fmfofprtvfj7lxprvgtq75ohi-story.html.

4   Neal Boudette, "'The Market Is Insane': Cars Are Sold Even Before They Hit the Lot," *The New York Times* (July 15, 2021), https://www.nytimes.com/2021/07/15/business/car-sales-chip-shortage.html.

5   Deb Gordon, "50% Of Americans Now Carry Medical Debt, A New Chronic Condition for Millions," *Forbes* (October 13, 2021), https://www.forbes.com/sites/debgordon/2021/10/13/50-of-americans-now-carry-medical-debt-a-new-chronic-condition-for-millions/?sh=5bcf4ee5e5dd.

6   The New York Federal Reserve Bank, Quarterly Report on Household Debt and Credit (November 9, 2021), https://www.newyorkfed.org/microeconomics/hhdc.html.

7   The work of the Debt Collective, the world's first debtor's union, has largely, but not exclusively, focused on student debt abolition: https://debtcollective.org/.

8   Melinda Zabritski, "State of the Automotive Finance Market, Q1 2021," Experian, https://www.experian.com/content/dam/noindex/na/us/automotive/finance-trends/q1-2021-state-of-auto-finance.pdf.

9   Human Rights Watch, "UAE: Foreign Debtor Trapped in Dire Circumstances" (May 10, 2021), https://www.hrw.org/news/2021/05/10/uae-foreign-debtor-trapped-dire-circumstances.

10   Human Rights Watch, "Saudi Arabia: Free Debtors from Prison" (2010), https://www.hrw.org/news/2010/11/02/saudi-arabia-free-debtors-prison.

11   Human Rights Watch, "Jordan: Widespread Imprisonment for Debt" (March 16, 2021), https://www.hrw.org/news/2021/03/16/jordan-widespread-imprisonment-debt.

12   See Conference of State Bank Supervisors, "50 State Survey of Consumer Finance Law" (November 19, 2020), https://www.csbs.org/50-state-survey-consumer-finance-laws.

13   Ryan Felton, "How America's Loophole-Ridden Auto Lending Laws Harm Consumers," *Consumer Reports* (December 6, 2021), https://www.consumerreports.org/car-financing/how-loophole-ridden-auto-lending-laws-harm-consumers-a3113489289/.

14   Adam Levitin analyzes the structure of the auto loan industry in "The Fast and the Usurious: Putting the Brakes on Auto Lending Abuses," Vol. 108, Issue 5, *Georgetown Law Journal* (May 2020), https://www.law.georgetown.edu/georgetown-law-journal/wp-content/uploads/sites/26/2020/05/Levitin_The-Fast-and-the-Usurious-Putting-the-Brakes-on-Auto-Lending-Abuses.pdf.

15   Ryan Felton, "The Devastating Loophole that Sticks Car Buyers With Interest Rates That Would Be Otherwise Illegal," *Jalopnik* (March 29, 2018), https://jalopnik.com/the-devastating-loophole-that-sticks-car-buyers-with-in-1823885194.

16   See Anne Fleming, "The Long History of 'Truth in Lending,'" *Journal of Policy History* 30, no. 2 (2018): 236–271.

17   Adam Tempkin, "Auto Lender Checked Income on 3% of Loans in Subprime Bond," *Bloomberg* (September 6, 2019), https://www.bloomberg.com/news/articles/2019-09-06/subprime-auto-lender-checked-income-on-just-3-of-loans-in-bond.

18   Gary Rivlin tells the story of Don Foss, the founder of Credit Acceptance, and "perhaps the richest used-car salesman in the history of the world," in "They Had Created This Remarkable System for Taking Every Last Dime From Their Customers," *Mother Jones* (May/June 2016), http:www.motherjones.com/politics/2016/04/car-subprime-bubble-auto-loans-credit-acceptance-don-foss/.

19   Bassem Banafa et al., "Reality Check: Credit Acceptance Corporation," *Plainsite* (December 13, 2017), https://www.plainsite.org/realitycheck/cacc1.pdf.

20   Zacks Equity Research, "Credit Acceptance Sued for Deceptive Auto-Lending
      Practices," *Nasdaq* (September 1, 2020), https://www.nasdaq.com/articles/credit-
      acceptance-sued-for-deceptive-auto-lending-practices-2020-09-01. In June 2020,
      the CFPB launched an official investigation, https://files.consumerfinance.gov/f/
      documents/cfpb_exhibits_credit-acceptance-corporation-redacted.pdf.

21   *Commonwealth of Massachusetts v. Credit Acceptance Corporation* (2020)
      https://buckleyfirm.com/sites/default/files/Buckley%20InfoBytes%20-%20
      Commonwealth%20of%20Mass.%20v.%20Credit%20Acceptance%20
      Corporation%20-%20complaint%20-%202020.08.28.pdf.

22   Gretchen Morgenson and Adiel Kaplan, "Many Auto Lenders Offered Deferrals
      to Borrowers During Covid. The Country's Biggest Subprime Lender Did Not,"
      NBC (April 30, 2021), https://www.nbcnews.com/business/consumer/many-auto-
      lenders-offered-deferrals-borrowers-during-covid-country-s-n1263194.

23   "Saxena White P.A. Files Securities Fraud Class Action Against Credit Acceptance
      Corporation," *Global NewsWire* (October 2, 2020), https://www.globenewswire.com/
      en/news-release/2020/10/02/2103131/0/en/Saxena-White-P-A-Files-Securities-
      Fraud-Class-Action-Against-Credit-Acceptance-Corporation.html.

24   Shahien Nasiripour,"Eisman's Biggest Short Is Subprime Lender Credit Acceptance,"
      Bloomberg (January 22, 2021), https://www.bloomberg.com/news/articles/2021-01-22/
      eisman-s-biggest-short-is-subprime-auto-lender-credit-acceptance.

25   Catherine Lutz and Anne Lutz Fernandez explain this industry maxim in
      Carjacked: The Culture of the Automobile and Its Effect on Our Lives (New York:
      Palgrave Macmillan, 2010), 62.

26   In June 2022, the Federal Trade Commission proposed new rule-making to protect
      consumers from these unscrupulous practices. "FTC Proposes Rule to Ban Junk
      Fees, Bait-and-Switch Tactics Plaguing Car Buyers," Federal Trade Commission
      (June 23, 2022), https://www.ftc.gov/news-events/news/press-releases/2022/06/
      ftc-proposes-rule-ban-junk-fees-bait-switch-tactics-plaguing-car-buyers.

27   Jim Akin, "What's the Average Length of a Car Loan?" Experian (October 3, 2020),
      https://www.experian.com/blogs/ask-experian/what-is-the-average-length-of-a-
      car-loan/.

28   Zabritski, "State of the Automotive Finance Market, Q1 2021."

29   Ivan Drury, "Negative Equity Is Surging During Coronavirus," *Edmund's* (2020),
      https://www.edmunds.com/industry/insights/negative-equity-is-surging-during-
      coronavirus.html.

30   According to the New Vehicle Price Index, a database of the BLS's Consumer Price
      Index, https://data.bls.gov/pdq/SurveyOutputServlet.

31   Zabritski, "State of the Automotive Finance Market, Q1 2021." Also see R. J. Cross
      et al., "Driving into Debt: The Hidden Costs of Risky Auto Loans to Consumers
      and Our Communities," Frontier Group and U.S. PIRG Education Fund (February
      2019), https://uspirg.org/sites/pirg/files/reports/WEB_USP_Driving-into-debt_
      Report_021219-v2.pdf.
32   Zabritski, "State of the Automotive Finance Market, Q1 2021."
33   Keeanga Yamahtta-Taylor, *Race for Profit: How Banks and the Real Estate Industry
      Undermined Black Homeownership* (Chapel Hill: University of North Carolina
      Press, 2019).
34   Dirk Breitschwerdt et al., "The Changing Aftermarket Game," McKinsey (June
      2019), https://www.mckinsey.com/~/media/McKinsey/Industries/Automotive%20
      and%20Assembly/Our%20Insights/The%20changing%20aftermarket%20
      game%20and%20how%20automotive%20suppliers%20can%20benefit%20
      from%20arising%20opportunities/The-changing-aftermarket-game.pdf.
35   "Single-Payment Vehicle Title Lending," Consumer Financial Protection Bureau
      (May 2016), https://files.consumerfinance.gov/f/documents/201605_cfpb_single-
      payment-vehicle-title-lending.pdf. A report from The Pew Charitable Trusts found
      repossession in 6 to 11 percent of all cases. "Auto Title Loans: Market Practices and
      Borrowers' Experiences" (2015), http://www.pewtrusts.org/~/media/assets/2015/03/
      autotitleloansreport.pdf.
36   On the topic of transportation equity, see Robert Bullard and Glenn Johnson, eds.,
      Just Transportation: Dismantling Race and Class Barriers to Mobility (Gabriola
      Island, Canada: New Society, 1997).
37   Ann Fleming surveys the history of paying more for "fringe finance" in *City of
      Debtors: A Century of Fringe Finance* (Cambridge: Harvard University Press, 2018).
38   National Consumer Law Center, "Racial Disparities in Auto Loan Markups"
      (June 2015), https://www.nclc.org/images/pdf/car_sales/ib-auto-dealers-racial_
      disparities.pdf.
39   Julia Angwin et al., *Car Insurance Companies Charge Higher Rates in Some Minority
      Neighborhoods,* Consumer Reports and ProPublica (April 21, 2017), https://www.
      consumerreports.org/consumer-protection/car-insurance-companies-charge-
      higher-rates-in-some-minority-neighborhoods/.
40   "2020 Year Review: Buy-Here, Pay-Here Trends," *Market Perspectives* (2020)
      https://sgcaccounting.com/Resources/BHPHBenchmarks2020.pdf; Ken Bensinger,
      "Investors Place Big Bets on Buy Here Pay Here Used-Car Dealers," *Los Angeles
      Times* (November 1, 2011), https://www.latimes.com/business/la-xpm-2011-nov-01-
      la-fi-buyhere-payhere-day-two-20111101-story.html.

41   Stephanie Lane, "The New Bill Collector Tactic: Jail Time," *Nolo,* https://www.nolo.com/legal-encyclopedia/the-new-bill-collector-tactic-jail-time.html.

42   Kevin McCoy, "Some U.S. Borrowers Jailed Over Civil Debts," *USA Today* (February 21, 2018), https://www.usatoday.com/story/money/2018/02/21/some-u-s-borrowers-jailed-over-civil-debts-aclu-report-shows/354867002/. See Jennifer Turner, *A Pound of Flesh: The Criminalization of Private Debt,* American Civil Liberties Union (2018), https://www.aclu.org/issues/smart-justice/mass-incarceration/criminalization-private-debt?redirect=issues/mass-incarceration/privatization-criminal-justice/pound-flesh.

43   Christopher L. Peterson and David McNeill, *Unwarranted: Small-Claims Court Arrest Warrants in Payday Loan Debt Collection,* Consumer Federation of America (February 2020), https://consumerfed.org/wp-content/uploads/2020/02/Payday-Lending-in-Small-Claims-Court.pdf.

44   Texas Appleseed, "Payday Businesses Unlawfully File 1,500 Criminal Complaints Against Borrowers to Collect Money" (December 2014), https://www.texasappleseed.org/sites/default/files/FINAL-PaydayComplaintRelease_Dec17.pdf.

45   Consumer Financial Protection Bureau, "Consumer Experiences with Debt Collection" (January 2017), https://files.consumerfinance.gov/f/documents/201701_cfpb_Debt-Collection-Survey-Report.pdf.

46   Andrew Ross, *Creditocracy and the Case for Debt Refusal* (New York: OR Books, 2014).

47   J. H. Crawford, *Carfree Cities,* (International Books, 2000) and *Carfree Design Manual* (International Books, 2009); John Urry et al., *The Little Book of Car Free Cities* (Imagination Lancaster, 2017), https://liveablecities.org.uk/sites/default/files/outcome_downloads/littlebookofcarfreecities.pdf.

48   Elizabeth Kneebone and Alan Berube, *Confronting Suburban Poverty in America* (Washington, DC: Brookings Institution, 2014).

49   Bureau of Labor Statistics, *Consumer Expenditures Report 2019* (January 2020), https://www.bls.gov/opub/reports/consumer-expenditures/2019/home.htm#chart4. See also Center for Neighborhood Technology, *Housing and Transportation Affordability Index,* https://htaindex.cnt.org/.

50   Shruti Vaidyanathan, "America's Transportation Energy Burden for Low-Income Households," American Council for an Energy-Efficient Economy (July 29, 2016).

51   The Pew Charitable Trusts, "How Income Volatility Interacts with American Families' Financial Security" (March 9, 2017), https://www.pewtrusts.org/en/research-and-analysis/issue-briefs/2017/03/how-income-volatility-interacts-with-american-families-financial-security.

Chapter Five

1   Justin George, "The Man with the Stolen Name," *The Marshall Project* (May 15, 2018), https://www.themarshallproject.org/2018/05/14/the-man-with-the-stolen-name; Mary Griffin, "Protecting One's Credit While in the Criminal Justice System," Consumer Financial Protection Bureau (April 28, 2016), https://www.consumerfinance.gov/about-us/blog/protecting-ones-credit-while-criminal-justice-system/; Christopher Zoukis, "Corrections Officials Stealing Prisoner Identities a Growing Problem," *Prison Legal News* (December 8, 2016), https://www.prisonlegalnews.org/news/2016/dec/8/corrections-officials-stealing-prisoners-identities-growing-problem/.

2   Alexandra Natapoff, *Punishment Without Crime*, p. 96.

3   As journalist Alana Semuels puts it, "licenses, to employers, signal responsibility." "No Driver's License, No Job," *The Atlantic* (June 15, 2016), https://www.theatlantic.com/business/archive/2016/06/no-drivers-license-no-job/486653/.

4   In 1990, George Bush signed the Solomon-Lautenberg amendment into law (attached to the 1991 transportation bill). It threatened to cut federal highway funding for states that failed to enact statutes automatically suspending the driver's license of anyone convicted of a drug offense. There was a provision for states to formally opt out of the policy, but nineteen states enacted new automatic suspension laws. Rebecca Beitsch, "States Reconsider Driver's License Suspensions for People with Drug Convictions," Pew Trust, (January 13 2017), https://www.pewtrusts.org/en/research-and-analysis/blogs/stateline/2017/01/31/states-reconsider-drivers-license-suspensions-for-people-with-drug-convictions.

5   Joshua Aiken, "Reinstating Common Sense: How Driver's License Suspensions for Drug Offenses Unrelated to Driving are Falling Out of Favor," Prison Policy Initiative (December 12, 2016) https://www.prisonpolicy.org/driving/national.html.

6   Free to Drive, https://www.freetodrive.org/about/.

7   Lynn Haney, "Incarcerated Fatherhood: The Entanglements of Child Support Debt and Mass Imprisonment," *American Journal of Sociology* 124, no. 1 (2018): 1–48.

8   Ethan May, "Holcomb Signs Bill Looking to Get Suspended Drivers Back on the Road Legally," *Indianapolis Star* (March 2, 2021), https://www.indystar.com/story/news/local/transportation/2021/03/02/indiana-drivers-license-suspensions-could-change-under-house-bill/4291634001/.

9   Indiana General Assembly, 2021 Session, House Bill 1199, http://iga.in.gov/legislative/2021/bills/house/1199#document-967c8589.

10 New York Economic Development Corporation, "New Yorkers and Their Cars" (April 5, 2018), https://edc.nyc/article/new-yorkers-and-their-cars.

11   Adie Tomer, "Where the Jobs Are: Employer Access to Labor by Transit," Metropolitan Policy Program, Brookings Institution (July 2012), https://www.brookings.edu/wp-content/uploads/2016/06/11-transit-labor-tomer-full-paper.pdf.

12   Sienna Kossman, "Poll: 4 in 10 Cosigners Lose Money," creditcards.com (June 6, 2016), https://www.creditcards.com/credit-card-news/co-signing-survey/.

13   See for example, Megan Flynn, "A Florida Cop Planted Meth on Random Drivers, Police Say. One Lost Custody of His Daughter," *Washington Post* (July 11, 2019), https://www.washingtonpost.com/nation/2019/07/11/florida-cop-meth-drugs-arrests-scandal/; Trevor Boyer, "Video Shows NYPD Officer Awkwardly Tossing Weed into Brooklyn Man's Car," *Gothamist* (October 18, 2019), https://gothamist.com/news/video-shows-nypd-officer-awkwardly-tossing-weed-into-brooklyn-mans-car; Justin Fenton, "Two Men Wrongfully Imprisoned After Fatal Crash Sue Baltimore Police: Will Seek $40 Million in Damages," *Baltimore Sun* (June 13, 2018), https://www.baltimoresun.com/news/crime/bs-md-ci-gttf-burley-lawsuit-20180612-story.html; Kelly Weil, "Baltimore Cops Caught Turning Off Body Cameras Before 'Finding' Drugs," *Daily Beast* (August 1, 2017); Tim O'Donnell, "Tapes Reveal Mount Vernon, New York, Police Officers Allegedly Fabricated Evidence, Made False Arrests," *The Week* (June 12, 2020), https://theweek.com/speedreads/917934/tapes-reveal-mount-vernon-new-york-police-officers-allegedly-fabricated-evidence-made-false-arrests; Jake Offenhartz, "NYPD Detectives with History of Alleged Misconduct Accused of Planting Drugs in Queens Apartment," *Gothamist* (July 25, 2017), https://gothamist.com/news/nypd-detectives-with-history-of-alleged-misconduct-accused-of-planting-drugs-in-queens-apartment; and Amir Vera and Eric Levenson, "Dozens of Convictions Tied to a Corrupt Chicago Cop Are Being Tossed," CNN (February 11, 2019), https://www.cnn.com/2019/02/11/us/chicago-convictions-dismissed-corrupt-cop/index.html.

14   For more on the socially extended costs of the prison commissary system, see Tommaso Bardelli, Zach Gillespie, and Thuy Linh Tu, "Blood From a Stone: How New York Prisons Force People to Pay for Their Own Incarceration," Prison Policy Initiative (October 27, 2021), https://www.prisonpolicy.org/blog/2021/10/27/ny_costs/.

15   Elana Confino-Pinzon, "Locked Up Far Away From Home: The Problem of Distance in New York State Prisons," *Brown Political Review* (March 30, 2019), https://brownpoliticalreview.org/2019/03/locked-far-away-home-problem-distance-new-york-state-prisons/.

16   Raymond Kluender, Neale Mahoney, Francis Wong, and Wesley Yin, "Medical Debt in the US, 2009–2020," *Journal of the American Medical Association,* 326, no. 3 (2021): 250–256.

Chapter Six

1   Ruha Benjamin, *Captivating Technology: Race, Carceral Technoscience, and Liberatory Imagination in Everyday Life* (Durham: Duke University Press, 2019), 2.

2   James B. Jacobs, *The Eternal Criminal Record* (Cambridge: Harvard University Press, 2015).

3   New York Department of Motor Vehicles, "Penalties for Alcohol or Drug-Related Violations," https://dmv.ny.gov/tickets/penalties-alcohol-or-drug-related-violations; Texas Department of Public Safety, "Administrative License Revocation Program," https://www.dps.texas.gov/section/driver-license/administrative-license-revocation-alr-program.

4   Louisiana Department of Revenue, "Frequently Asked Questions," https://revenue.louisiana.gov/faq/Details/1273#:~:text=Revised%20Statute%2047%3A296.2%20authorizes,that%20is%20final%20and%20nonappealable.&text=If%20the%20assessment%20is%20based,return%20for%20the%20tax%20period; New York State Department of Taxation and Finance, "Driver's License Suspension," https://www.tax.ny.gov/enforcement/collections/driver-license-susp.htm.

5   Ohio Bureau of Motor Vehicles, "Suspensions and Reinstatements," https://www.bmv.ohio.gov/susp-court-license-forfeiture.aspx; https://codes.ohio.gov/ohio-revised-code/section-4510.22.

6   South Dakota Department of Public Safety, "Revoked or Suspended Licenses," https://dps.sd.gov/driver-licensing/south-dakota-licensing-information/revoked-or-suspended.

7   John B. Mitchell and Kelly Kunsch, "Of Driver's Licenses and Debtor's Prison," *Seattle Journal for Social Justice* 4, no. 1 (2005): 439.

8   "Driven Deeper Into Debt: Unrealistic Repayment Options Hurt Low-Income Court Debtors," Legal Aid and Justice Center, Virginia School of Law (May 4, 2016).

9   Keesha Middlemass and Jyl Josephson, "Child Support Enforcement, Poverty, and the Creation of the New Debtor's Prison," *Feminist Formations* 33, no. 1 (2021): 96–116.

10   Alice Speri, "NYPD Gang Database Expanded by 70 Percent Under Mayor Bill De Blasio," *The Intercept* (June 11, 2018), https://theintercept.com/2018/06/11/new-york-gang-database-expanded-by-70-percent-under-mayor-bill-de-blasio/; Jonathan Blitzer, "How Gang Victims Are Labelled as Gang Suspects," *The New Yorker* (January 23, 2018), https://www.newyorker.com/news/news-desk/how-gang-victims-are-labelled-as-gang-suspects?utm_source=NYR_REG_GATE; Melissa del Bosque, "Immigration Officials Use Secretive Gang Databases to Deny Migrant

Asylum Claims," ProPublica (July 8, 2019), https://www.propublica.org/article/immigration-officials-use-secretive-gang-databases-to-deny-migrant-asylum-claims; Anita Chabria, Kevin Rector, and Cindy Chang, "California Bars Police From Using LAPD Records in Gang Database. Critics Want it Axed," *Los Angeles Times* (July 14, 2020), https://www.latimes.com/california/story/2020-07-14/california-bars-police-from-using-lapd-records-in-gang-database-as-scandal-widens; Ali Winston, "Prosecutors are using Gang Laws to Criminalize Protest," *The Appeal* (September 1, 2020), https://theappeal.org/gang-laws-criminalize-protest/.

11   Congressional Research Service, *The Child Support Enforcement Program: A Legislative History* (March 21, 2016), R 44423, 25.

12   Ibid, 28.

13   As ICE itself acknowledged in response to a 2016 FOIA request from the National Immigration Law Center, there is no federal policy governing such interagency access to DMV data. National Immigration Law Center, "Documents Obtained Under Freedom of Information Act: How U.S. Immigration and Customs Enforcement and State Motor Vehicle Departments Share Information" (May 2016), https://www.nilc.org/issues/drivers-licenses/ice-dmvs-share-information/.

14   Mariah Kauder, "Out of the Shadows: Regulating Access to Driver's License Databases by Government Agencies," *Drake Law Review* 69, no. 2 (2021): 463–485.

15   Keith Gierlack, Shara Williams, Tom LaTourrette, James Anderson, Lauren Mayer, and Johanna Zmud, *License Plate Readers for Law Enforcement: Opportunities and Obstacles,* Rand Corporation (2014), 12. ALPRs are also an integral part of the militarized expansion of the US southern border's carceral apparatus. See Mizue Aizeki, Geoffrey Boyce, Todd Miller, Joseph Nevins, and Miriam Ticktin, *Smart Borders or a Humane World?* The Immigrant Defense Project's Surveillance, Tech & Immigration Policing Project and the Transnational Institute (October 2021), https://www.immigrantdefenseproject.org/smart-borders-or-a-humane-world/.

16   Electronic Frontier Foundation, "Street Level Surveillance, Automated License Plate Readers (ALPRS)," https://www.eff.org/pages/automated-license-plate-readers-alpr.

17   International Association of Chiefs of Police, *Privacy Impact Assessment Report for the Utilization of License Plate Readers* (September 2009), https://www.theiacp.org/sites/default/files/all/k-m/LPR_Privacy_Impact_Assessment.pdf.

18   Angel Diaz and Rachel Levinson-Waldman, "Automatic License Plate Readers: Legal Status and Policy Recommendations for Law Enforcement Use," Brennan Center for Justice (September 10, 2020), https://www.brennancenter.org/our-work/

research-reports/automatic-license-plate-readers-legal-status-and-policy-recomm endations#footnote8_6lmcamx.

19 Department of Homeland Security, *Privacy Impact Assessment for the Acquisition and Use of License Plate Reader (LPR) Data from a Commercial Service*, DHS reference No. DHS/ICE/PIA-O39(b) (May 21, 2021).

20 David Maass, "Data Driven 2: California Dragnet—New Dataset Shows Scale of Vehicle Surveillance in the Golden State," Electronic Frontier Foundation (April 22, 2021), https://www.eff.org/deeplinks/2021/04/data-driven-2-california-dragnet-new-dataset-shows-scale-vehicle-surveillance.

21 Adam Goldman and Matt Apuzzo, "NYPD Defends Tactics Over Mosque Spying; Records Reveal New Details On Muslim Surveillance," *Huffington Post* (February 24, 2012), https://www.huffpost.com/entry/nypd-defends-tactics-over_n_1298997.

22 National Conference of State Legislatures, "Automated License Plate Readers: State Statutes," https://www.ncsl.org/research/telecommunications-and-information-technology/state-statutes-regulating-the-use-of-automated-license-plate-readers-alpr-or-alpr-data.aspx.

23 Sarah Holder and Fola Akinnibi, "Suburbs of Surveillance," *Bloomberg City Lab* (August 4, 2021), https://www.bloomberg.com/news/features/2021-08-04/surveillance-startup-brings-police-tech-to-neighborhoods.

24 Diaz and Levinson-Waldman, "Report: Automatic License Plate Readers."

25 Jessica Porter, "Aurora Police Detain Black Family After Mistaking Their Vehicle as Stolen," *The Denver Channel* (August 5, 2020), https://www.thedenverchannel.com/news/local-news/aurora-police-detain-black-family-after-mistaking-their-vehicle-as-stolen.

26 Lily Hay Newman, "Internal Docs Show How ICE Gets Surveillance Help From Local Cops, *Wired* (August 13, 2019), https://www.wired.com/story/ice-license-plate-surveillance-vigilant-solutions/.

27 Erin Markowitz, "Pay This Fee or Go to Jail: How License Plate Scanner Vigilant Solutions Makes Money in Texas," *International Business Times* (February 3, 2016), https://www.ibtimes.com/pay-fee-or-go-jail-how-license-plate-scanner-vigilant-solutions-makes-money-texas-2290835.

28 David Maass, "'No Cost' License Plate Readers Are Turning Texas Police into Mobile Debt Collectors," Electronic Frontier Foundation (January 26, 2016), https://www.eff.org/deeplinks/2016/01/no-cost-license-plate-readers-are-turning-texas-police-mobile-debt-collectors-and.

29 Axon, another major provider of law enforcement technologies, was pressured to convene an AI Ethics Board (https://www.axon.com/company/ai-and-policing-technology-ethics) to ensure that its face-matching and ALPR

products are developed to benefit communities, and not profile them. NYU Law School's Policing Project is represented on the board, and contributed to its most recent 2020 End of Year Report, at https://static1.squarespace.com/static/58a33e881b631bc60d4f8b31/t/603d65a9d4ef6e4f9632b342/1614636462250/Axon+AI+Ethics+Board+2020+EOY+Report.pdf.

30   See the DRN website, https://drndata.com/.

31   ACLU staff attorney Nate Wessler, quoted in Joseph Cox, "This Company Built a Private Surveillance Network, We Tracked Someone With It," *Motherboard* (September 17, 2019), https://www.vice.com/en/article/ne879z/i-tracked-someone-with-license-plate-readers-drn.

32   Kurt Opsahl, "EFF Responds to Vigilant Solutions Accusations about EFF ALPR Report" (July 12, 2018), https://www.eff.org/deeplinks/2018/07/eff-responds-vigilant-solutions-accusations-about-eff-alpr-report.

33   Electronic Privacy Information Center, "The Drivers Privacy Protection Act (DPPA) and the Privacy of Your State Motor Vehicle Record," https://epic.org/privacy/drivers/.

34   Angela Brauer, "Records Show the Indiana BMV Has Been Selling People's Personal Information," CBS 4, Indianapolis (November 18, 2021), https://cbs4indy.com/news/records-show-the-indiana-bmv-has-been-selling-peoples-personal-information/; New York State Department of Motor Vehicles, "Sharing Your Information," https://dmv.ny.gov/dmv-records/sharing-your-information.

35   Matt Moore, "The DMV Sells Your Information, Makes Millions," WYFF, Greenville, South Carolina (July 3, 2018), https://www.wyff4.com/article/the-dmv-sells-your-information-makes-millions/22520650#.

36   Adam Walser, "I-Team: Florida DMV Sells Your Personal Information to Private Companies, Marketing Firms," WFTS, Tampa Bay (July 10, 2019), https://www.abcactionnews.com/news/local-news/i-team-investigates/i-team-florida-dmv-sells-your-personal-information-to-private-companies-marketing-firms. See also "CBS 11 Investigates: State Sells Personal Information and You Can't Opt Out," CBS 11, Dallas Fort Worth (February 11, 2013), https://dfw.cbslocal.com/2013/02/11/cbs-11-investigates-your-personal-information-for-sale-you-cant-opt-out/; Joseph Cox, "DMVs Are Selling Your Data to Private Investigators," *Motherboard* (September 6, 2019), https://www.vice.com/en/article/43kxzq/dmvs-selling-data-private-investigators-making-millions-of-dollars.

37   Gopal Ratnam, "Your Car is Watching You: Who Owns the Data?" *Roll Call* (April 9, 2019), https://www.rollcall.com/2019/04/09/your-car-is-watching-you-who-owns-the-data/.

38   Elaine Povitch, "Late Payment? A 'Kill Switch' Can Strand You and Your Car," Stateline, Pew Charitable Trust (November 27, 2018), https://www.pewtrusts.org/en/research-and-analysis/blogs/stateline/2018/11/27/late-payment-a-kill-switch-can-strand-you-and-your-car; Michael Corkery and Jessica Silver-Greenberg, "Miss a Payment? Good Luck Moving that Car," *The New York Times* (September 24, 2014), https://dealbook.nytimes.com/2014/09/24/miss-a-payment-good-luck-moving-that-car/?ref=dealbook.

39   Mikella Hurley and Julius Adebayo, "Credit Scoring in the Era of Big Data," *Yale Journal of Law and Technology* 18, no. 1 (2016): 148–216.

40   Kenneth Brevoort, Philip Grimm, and Michelle Kambara, "Credit Invisibles and the Unscored," *Cityscape: A Journal of Policy Development and Research* 18, no. 2 (2016): 9–34.

41   Mikella Hurley and Julius Adebayo, "Credit Scoring in the Era of Big Data," *Yale Journal of Law and Technology* 18, no. 1 (2016): 157.

42   Quentin Hardy, "Just the Facts. Yes, All of Them," *The New York Times* (March 25, 2012), https://archive.nytimes.com/query.nytimes.com/gst/fullpage-9A0CE7DD153 CF936A15750C0A9649D8B63.html.

43   Barbara Kiviat, "Credit Scoring in the United States," *Economic Sociology* 21, no. 1 (November 2019): 37.

44   Hurley and Adebayo, "Credit Scoring in the Era of Big Data."

45   Akos Rona-Tas, "The Off-Label Use of Consumer Credit Ratings," *Historical Social Research/Historische Sozialforschung* 42, no. 1 (2017): 52–76.

Conclusion

1   IAA Mobility 2021, https://www.iaa.de/de/mobility.

2   Transit Protocol, "What is Mobility as a Service?" Medium (January 18, 2019), https://medium.com/@transitprotocol/what-is-mobility-as-a-service-672259066c87. McKinsey's Center for Future Mobility summarizes the corporate vision in "The Future of Mobility is at Our Doorstep" (2020), https://www.mckinsey.com/~/media/McKinsey/Industries/Automotive%20and%20Assembly/Our%20Insights/The%20future%20of%20mobility%20is%20at%20our%20doorstep/The-future-of-mobility-is-at-our-doorstep.ashx. For a fuller commentary, see Todd Litman, *New Mobilities: Smart Planning for Emerging Transportation Technologies* (Washington, DC: Island Press, 2021).

3   Norman Bel Geddes, the designer of the driverless Futurama, centerpiece of GM's
     landmark Highways and Horizons pavilion at the 1939 World's Fair, summed up
     the technocratic impatience with human error and traffic irritation with a simple
     slogan: "Eliminate the Human Factor in Driving." Quoted in Dan Albert, *Are We
     There Yet? The American Automobile Past, Present, and Driverless* (New York:
     Norton, 2019). 246–49.

4   Ruha Benjamin, *Race After Technology: Abolitionist Tools for the New Jim Code*
     (Cambridge, UK: Polity, 2019); Wendy Hui Kyong Chun and Alex Barnett,
     *Discriminating Data: Correlation, Neighborhoods, and the New Politics of
     Recognition* (Cambridge: MIT Press, 2021).

5   Simone Browne, *Dark Matters: On the Surveillance of Blackness* (Durham: Duke
     University Press, 2015).

6   See Thomas Kowalick, *Black Box: What's Under Your Hood* (MICAH, 2005).

7   Anthony Townsend anticipates the financialization of mobility in *Ghost Roads:
     Beyond the Driverless Car* (New York: Norton, 2020), 161–83. Paris Marx skewers
     the "future of mobility" hype in *Road to Nowhere: What Silicon Valley Gets Wrong
     about the Future of Transportation* (New York: Verso, 2022).

8   Cameron Krueger and Tiffany Johnson, *Financing the Future of Mobility; Auto
     Finance in the Evolving Transportation Ecosystem* (Deloitte, 2016).

9   *Blueprint for Autonomous Urbanism*, produced by the National Association of City
     Transportation Officials (2019, second edition), https://nacto.org/publication/bau2.

10   The editors of the *Journal of Law and Mobility* have made these concerns central
     to a new Law and Mobility Initiative, focused on the relationship between
     transportation technology and modern slavery; https://futurist.law.umich.edu/
     introducing-the-new-law-and-mobility-initiative/.

11   Angela Davis, *Are Prisons Obsolete?* (New York: Seven Stories Press, 2003).

12   For example, People for Mobility Justice is a Los Angeles–based organization
     serving BIPOC communities, https://www.peopleformobilityjustice.org/about.
     Also active in the same urban space is The Untokening Collective, http://www.
     untokening.org/. See also Mimi Sheller's expansive survey of the politics of
     mobility across borders, *Mobility Justice, The Politics of Movement in an Age of
     Extremes* (New York: Verso, 2018).

13   *Report on the Economic Well-Being of U.S. Households in 2018*, Board of Governors
     of the Federal Reserve System (May 2019), https://www.federalreserve.gov/
     publications/files/2018-report-economic-well-being-us-households-201905.pdf.

About the Authors

Julie Livingston teaches in the departments of social and cultural analysis and history at New York University, where she is also a founding member of the NYU Prison Education Program Research Lab. She is the recipient of numerous awards, including a 2013 MacArthur Foundation Fellowship. Her most recent book is *Self-Devouring Growth: A Planetary Parable as Told from Southern Africa.*

Andrew Ross is a social activist and professor at NYU, where he teaches in the department of social and cultural analysis and the Prison Education Program. A cofounder of the Debt Collective, he is a contributor to *The Guardian, The New York Times, The Nation,* and *Al Jazeera,* and the author or editor of twenty-five books, including, most recently, *Sunbelt Blues: The Failure of American Housing.*

CPSIA information can be obtained
at www.ICGtesting.com
Printed in the USA
JSHW081519261022
32053JS00006B/5